COGNITIVE BEHAVIORAL THERAPY

11 Simple CBT Techniques to Strengthen Self-Awareness and Combat Negativity

Michael B. Stump

The Mentor Bucket

The Mentor Bucket

© Copyright 2021 - All rights reserved.

It is not legal to reproduce, duplicate, or transmit any part of this document in either electronic means or in printed format. Recording of this publication is strictly prohibited and any storage of this document is not allowed unless with written permission from the publisher except for the use of brief quotations in a book review.

TABLE OF CONTENTS

Preface 5

Introduction 13

Chapter One: Mental-Health Issues and the Role of Cognitive Behavioral Therapy (CBT) 17

Chapter Two: Safety Plan 39

Chapter Three: Technique 1– Cognitive Restructuring 49

Chapter Four: Technique 2 – Bursting Mental Distortions 59

Chapter Five: Technique 3 – Write it Down 79

Chapter Six: Technique 4 – Exposure and Response Prevention 90

Chapter Seven: Technique 5 – Relax 103

Chapter Eight: Technique 6 – Have Fun 119

Chapter Nine: Technique 7 – Testing the Beliefs . 127

Chapter Ten: Technique 8 – Role-Playing 135

Chapter Eleven: Technique 9 – Simply Break It Down 145

Chapter Twelve: Technique 10 – Mindfulness 152

Chapter Thirteen: Technique 11 – Play the Entire Script.. 162

Final Words.. 168

PREFACE

As usual, I was awake at the crack of dawn. If my mind had been clear, I would have appreciated the quietness of the morning, the fresh air and the beauty that comes with the first light of the day. However, I did not want to get out of bed. No, I wasn't sleepy. I could not even remember the last night I had had more than a few hours of sleep despite being in bed by 9:30 p.m. each night.

That Wednesday morning should have been an exciting day for me. I was finally receiving the award for being the top CEO in the pharmaceutical industry. I should have been excited and proud for accomplishing such a feat at only 38 years old. I was at the top of the world, leading the most promising and innovative company in the country, yet there I was, sad and crushed.

I glanced at my wife who was doing her yoga on a mat on the balcony. I couldn't help but appreciate her beauty yet notice that the joy and light in her were fading. She was a bubbly girl, confident and ambitious with sparkling eyes. What remained now was a shell of the woman I met and married. She looked in my direction and upon seeing me, looked away. The few seconds that our eyes met, I saw the heartbreak, the suppressed anger and hatred.

I knew that look; I had lived through that look. It was the same look my mother had when she looked at my father. For a moment, the world stood still, my eyes opened, and my mind was clear. I walked to the mirror and looked at myself. What had I become? My wife hated me, my children feared me, yet, on the outside, I was the most celebrated man. As I looked keenly at my face, I noticed my hollow eyes devoid of any emotion, I hated myself.

On the day I was to receive a prestigious award, the day I had the stamp of success, and the day I had a dinner invitation from the president, I felt worthless. I felt empty and broken inside. Most times, when I felt weak, I would focus my energy on my work or anger. Anger gave me the strength I needed. For once in my life, I did not yield to anger; there wasn't enough left within me.

As I sat on the edge of the bed, tears began rolling down my cheeks. My heart broke, my life seemed empty as a lie. Only one question was on my mind: "How did I get here?"

My mind went to that young energetic boy running in the fields, feeling free. He could hear his mother calling for him to go home have a meal. She did not have to call twice. Her food had a reputation in the village of being the best. As he approached the house, he could see his sisters helping to set the table while his younger brother played on the mat. Just as the last fork found its place on the dinner table, he heard his father pull up the drive. The entire household seemed to run outside to welcome the man of the house. They all looked forward to their father's arrival. Not only were there gifts but also stories and an evening filled with laughter and counsel.

Everything changed one evening. Father came home, but there were no stories or gifts, everything was solemn, and the young boy knew that something had changed. He, however, could not expect the magnitude of the change.

I quickly collected my thoughts, wiped away my tears and went into the bathroom to get ready for the day. Standing in the shower, I let the water flow and wash my feelings off, cleanse me of the burden I carried and make me free. Almost half an hour later I heard a soft knock on the door, I knew that my wife was wondering why I was taking so long. I was known as a stickler for time, and everything had to happen at a particular time, otherwise, there would be hell to pay if my tea was not at the right temperature.

At the office, everyone was excited about the award. Despite the excitement, there was something in the air, the same thing I felt at home: fear and tension. The staff came forward to offer congratulatory messages, but I kicked everyone out. I could not take it anymore. On my magnificent table, I broke down for the first time in years. I bared my soul, I felt so little, defeated, heavy, lost and alone...alone among hundreds of people. I sent a text to my wife asking her to come. She did not respond, and I knew I had pushed her away too.

In the bottom cabinet, there were some pills, the ones Dr. Elena gave me to help me calm down and, after the first two, I decided I needed more calm today than any other day. Filling my hand with the white pills, I drowned them with the waiting cup of tea and relaxed waiting for the calmness to set in. After all, it was better to end it all and have a peaceful life.

When I came to, I saw my wife seated beside me crying. She still looked beautiful, and I couldn't help but tell her. Relief filled her face as she called for the doctor. She held my hand throughout the examination and repeatedly whispered that everything could be OK.

The doctor recommended that I go for therapy, which I adamantly refused. Therapy was for the weak.

Upon discharge, my wife took me home. That evening, she served the tea outside in the garden. It was a beautiful day. She looked into my eyes with concern and said she was listening. The girl can be stubborn when not scared. She urged me to talk to her and let out the devils within. The brokenness within me rose again.

With tears streaming from my eyes, I told her of my dad losing his job and slowly sinking into fits of anger. He felt incapable of taking care of us and instead of looking for something to do, another job, he accumulated anger at the world. He became a closet drunkard but maintained a face outside. My mother's family stepped in and set up a sweets shop for her, which my father claimed ownership, but hardly ever helped. With my mother taking care of the bills, my father got even angrier. He may have felt inadequate. That is when the abuse began. He would hit my mother so hard we were forced to go help her, lest he killed her. We were not spared of the beatings, either. He kept warning us to stay away from his fights with my mother.

The more I grew, the more I could not watch my mother get battered and my father praised for being an influential person in the community. I vowed to work hard and have so much money that I would never be like him. I focused my energy on school, made good grades and landed a scholarship. My mother and I were grateful, and she knew there was hope for the family.

One day I came home from the university and, as usual, my father, in his angry drunken state, descended on my mother with kicks and blows for serving him a cold dinner. I got in between them and, in the process, pushed him. He fell to the ground and hurt his head. He said that he would get his revenge. In the morning, mother did not wake up...it was all my fault.

We sat there, in the garden seat, sobbing. My wife hugged me and asked me why I carried that around for all those years. I told her I felt guilty for the death of my mother and, as a man, society did not allow me to show emotion or even talk about such things. Talking about pain and crying were for the weak. Men did not do so. She urged me to go for therapy and would walk through the journey with me. Although doubtful, I agreed. I was tired of being sick, tired, guilty and angry.

Initially, I thought therapy to be a waste of time. However, over time I have found myself. Having to look deep inside you will open your eyes to life as is. I have gotten an opportunity to face the pain inside me and chart the path for my life from a place of peace. I no longer need sleeping pills as the nightmares are gone. I have become a present father and a loving husband. I am still successful, and my business is growing each day thanks to me being more accommodating. I now receive innovative ideas from my staff without them worrying about being shouted at. I have gotten time to properly mourn for my mother and forgive my father. I chose not to give my father the space to turn me into him. I have control of my emotions and am no longer depressed. I am reborn.

Throughout my therapy, I realized that anyone can battle any form of mental illness. There is no particular way that people with depression or anxiety look. I was the successful, depressed CEO who never showed any signs of weakness, yet I was sick. I have met happy people who cry themselves to sleep. Most importantly, I have practically learned about different ways that you can apply to defeat mental issues, like depression and anxiety. I did it, and you can do it, too!

Having been there and successfully gone through therapy despite having been in denial and feeling lost and hopeless, I am willing to share with you what worked for me. I must confess that prior to Cognitive Behavioral Therapy (CBT), I went through other forms of treatment, including medication, but that did not help. I felt worse once the effect of the pills wore off, and it was through that medication that I saw a way to end my life. My journey through CBT was not easy in the beginning. Having to look inside was especially difficult, but I learned, walked the path and healed. I can help you get the peace and healing you crave. Together, we can walk from the depths of hopelessness and darkness and into the light and hope. I will offer simple and practical techniques that you can apply as part of your daily activities to ensure that you get better, find your peace and cement your place in the society. I am looking forward to the emergence of a strong, confident and positive person who spreads joy and peace to those around him—that is you.

INTRODUCTION

We all have some dark days when we lack energy and feel down. You must have experienced that, especially, in these challenging times and the economy slumping. Those days are the worst; even interacting with other people is tiresome. Now, consider feeling like this every other day and having to carry on with life? Sad as it is, it is what is happening to millions of people all over the world. The World Health Organization in 2019 estimated that 264 million people globally were depressed. Please note this was before the pandemic and that is depression only. In total, about 790 million people in the world suffer from one form of mental disorder or another.

Yet, mental health is not considered as important as physical health. If you hurt your leg today, the entire family would drive you to the emergency room. On the other hand, if they saw you slowly slipping away, moody and losing interest in life, they would assume that you would simply snap back. The only time most people will take action is when physical evidence appears, such as wounds from self-hurt or hurting others. As a society, we want to see evidence that the other person is sick, something like fever or convulsion. We are convinced that the smiling girl cannot be sick or the high-flying athlete cannot be depressed. How can they be sick when they are so beautiful, energetic and successful? Despite signs, like unexplainable mood swings, panic attacks and visible anxiety, mental illness is not accorded the necessary weight.

Have you been battling any form of mental illness? Do you have someone close to you going through depression or anxiety? Well, no matter how misunderstood you feel, you can have some peace in the knowledge that you are not alone. I have been there, and although my situation may be different from yours, I pulled through, and so can you.

In this book, we look at the overview of mental health and some of the mental illnesses that are increasing each day. The focus, however, will be on the techniques that you can apply to deal with mental issues. In particular, we will look at simple techniques, such as journaling and testing your beliefs. The aim of this book is to help you go through the process, even at home. I will offer practical advice, in a simple manner, on some of the methods that I used in my journey that proved to be effective.

If you or someone you know needs to face the muddy grounds within them, to address those underlying issues, swim through the murky waters to the clean water, then this is the book. There is no need to wallow in pain anymore. You do not have to keep being weighed down by what you carry; you can offload and have some rest. Don't bother picking up that baggage again; you can throw it away and enjoy the life that you are blessed to have. Joy and peace are for everyone, not a chosen few. Not only can you have life, but life in abundance.

You are not alone. This book is for you who feels like you are carrying the weight of the world on your shoulders. It is particularly tailored for you who feel those suicidal thoughts creeping in and feel so overwhelmed and powerless. Yet, this book is also for that person that feels down and has yet to pin it down to a reason. Whatever mental issue you are facing, this book is a resource to take you step by step through the healing and self-discovery process using simple cognitive behavioral therapy techniques. In addition to these, the book also targets caregivers to help them give care and hope to the mentally ill. They say information is power. Being equipped with the information in this book not only contributes to their improved knowledge but places them in a better position to deal with their patients.

The time to cry yourself to sleep is over. Now is not the time to entertain those harmful thoughts. You can get out of this. You can breathe again and enjoy life. Yes, you can be in control of your mind and actions.

> *"The happiness of your life depends on the quality of your thoughts."*
> — Marcus Aurelius

CHAPTER ONE

Mental-Health Issues and the Role of Cognitive Behavioral Therapy (CBT)

For a long time, therapy was a reserve of a few people who were mainly considered to be 'mad'. Having to see a therapist meant that you were losing your mind, or you were a weakling. Normal people faced and dealt with issues. They went through hiding any mental issues because society was not prepared to handle them. However, over the years, mental-health issues have begun to gain recognition and be treated as illnesses rather than a weakness.

The challenge with mental illnesses is that they are not easy to detect. I am certain that everyone at one point or another has experienced anxiety. Times like right before an interview, while waiting for results, on a first date, or when experiencing other illnesses. Most of us get panic attacks once in a while, and those blue days do come. Sometimes it's a whole week that is blue or even several weeks. At what point is it just a bad day, and when does it graduate to a health concern? Let us see what is normal, then we can tell what is abnormal.

Mental Health

Each day you wake up, you can expect to feel, think and act. How you do so is determined by the state of your mental health. If two people are hurt by someone, one may complain and walk away while another may draw a gun and shoot. How healthy your mental health is determines how well you can make choices, handle stress and relate to other people. Therefore, mental health is your psychological, social and emotional well-being.

Taking care of your mental health is important at each stage of life, be it childhood, adolescence or adulthood. If anything happens at any point in life that destabilizes the wellness of the mind, you could start experiencing mental-health problems. You cannot outgrow mental-health issues. As you live and feel pity or judge others who have such issues, remember that you are not past them. Each day presents the potential for joining millions of people suffering from mental-health disorders. Do not worry though; it is now easier to detect mental disorders and even to treat them. Besides, you can put in measures to prevent mental-health issues.

If you have the bubbly and outgoing neighbour who now hardly goes out or even bothers to shower, you must wonder how she got there. Well, there are many factors that contribute to mental-health problems. Some of these include:

- Life experiences like abuse, loss, or trauma
- Biological factors like brain chemistry or genes
- Family history: People who come from lineages of people with mental-health problems are inclined to develop similar problems.

What are Mental-Health Disorders?

They are also referred to as mental-health illnesses, and they include a wide range of conditions that affect your behavior, mood or thinking. Some of the most common ones include anxiety disorders, depression, addictive behaviors, eating disorders and schizophrenia.

While it is normal to experience mental-health concerns from time to time, it becomes an illness when the signs and symptoms result in frequent stress and hinder your ability to function. Experiencing anxiety because of a test or a problem does not translate to a mental disorder. However, when the anxiety becomes so frequent that you can no longer undertake your daily activities with ease, then there is a problem.

Mental-health disorders have the ability to make your life a living hell. They can make you unproductive, dirty and unable to form and sustain relationships with others. They can ruin your family and career. Signs and symptoms of different disorders vary from one person to another and come in varying intensities.

Who is suffering?

If you are suffering from one or more mental-health disorders, you may be a difficult person to please, but at least have some peace in the knowledge that you are not alone. The World Bank estimates that at least 10% of the people in the world are affected. Furthermore, about 20% of children and adolescents have to deal with some type of mental illness. Countries that have violence and conflict have an estimated 22% of their population suffering from mental disorders.

Depression is the major mental-health disorder and affects about 264 million people, with a majority of them being women, as per a WHO report in 2019. About 54 million people suffer from bipolar disorder, 20 million are affected by schizophrenia and a further 50 million people have dementia. You can tell from the data that mental disorders are not a preserve of a few.

Sadly, the population of people suffering from these illnesses is increasing due to economic factors and the changing times.

Are you affected?

Many people suffer for a long time from mental disorders before they are diagnosed and put on treatment. In my case, I had to reach a breaking point to take action. The challenge is that the symptoms are attributable to life's pressures and normal feelings and that makes it difficult to point them out. If you are unsure, here are some of the common symptoms of mental illnesses. Please note that these can vary from person to person as per the circumstances and disorder.

Many people with mental-health problems experience sadness or feeling down, reduced ability to concentrate, confused thinking and extreme mood swings. They can be over the moon one moment and completely broken the next. Excessive worries and fears are common, as well as withdrawal from activities and friends. If you have that one friend who is suddenly very busy even for coffee, you may want to check up on him.

Other symptoms include low energy, tiredness and sleep problems, as well as an inability to deal with stress and daily problems, which can lead to hallucinations, paranoia and detachment from reality. The person may also experience trouble relating to people and situations or become hostile, angry and violent. You may also notice changes in eating habits and sex drives, as well as destructive thoughts. Mental disorders may be accompanied by alcohol and drug use. There is more. Occasionally, the person may experience physical problems, like back pain, stomach pains and headaches.

Looking at all these symptoms that zap the life out of a person, it is evident that mental illnesses deserve to be taken seriously. If you or a person close to you are exhibiting one of these symptoms, it is best to see your physician or a mental-health professional. Most mental illnesses get worse if left untreated, and it is best to get an early diagnosis. If things seem thick, and you feel like you're on the verge of harming yourself or others, don't be like me. Call 911 or any emergency number. Remember that no matter how bad you are feeling, your life matters.

Diagnosis of Mental illness

Often the people affected by mental illness do not realize that they have a problem because most of the symptoms are feelings we all experience, like anger, sadness and anxiety. Therefore, when a person begins to note increased frequency and intensity of these symptoms, it is best to go for diagnosis.

The diagnosis process may involve a physical exam to ensure that the symptoms are not caused by a physical problem. Laboratory tests are also done to ensure the proper functioning of the body system. Lab tests may include screening for drugs or thyroid function, among others. Finally, a psychological evaluation is done. The health practitioner talks to the patient about thoughts, feelings, symptoms and behavior patterns.

Most mental illnesses display a similar array of symptoms, and it may be an uphill task to get the right diagnosis. There is a need to take time and effort in digging deeper into the symptoms, thoughts and behavior patterns to get the right diagnosis.

Treatment methods

If diagnosis shows that there is a mental disorder, the preferred method of treatment will depend on the mental illness in question, how severe it is and what works best for you. I know some people who can barely swallow a pill, yet others even go a step ahead to self-medicate and abuse pills. There is also the question of how controllable the condition is, which will determine the treatment team to bring on board. For example, if you are suffering from something mild, you can undergo the treatment by yourself. However, if you have, for instance, been diagnosed with Type 1 Bipolar, then your treatment team may need to be larger than your primary care provider.

A holistic treatment team includes the primary care doctor, nurse, physician assistant, psychiatrist, pharmacist, psychotherapist, social worker and family members. You remain to be the most important member of this team.

Ideally, you should be presented with different options available for treatment and, together with the health care professional, choose one that suits you best. Whatever method you settle for, ensure that you fully understand all the benefits and risks that come with it. Some of the available methods include:

1. Medications

With mental illnesses, medications are hardly ever curative. Instead, they help to alleviate the severity of the symptoms. For example, if you are suffering from Post-Traumatic Stress Disorder and cannot sleep due to recurring nightmares, you can be given sleeping pills to help you sleep better. However, these pills do not address the trauma that is causing a lack of sleep.

Do not think that you will not need medications. They help to improve the effectiveness of other treatment methods, like psychotherapy. Some of the medications used are:

- Antidepressants, for anxiety, depression and related conditions.
- Mood-stabilizing medications that help with bipolar disorders.
- Anti-anxiety medications that treat panic attacks and anxiety disorders.
- Antipsychotic medications for conditions, like schizophrenia and also help with bipolar disorders and depression.

2. Residential/Hospital treatment programs

In some cases, the mental illness is so severe that you have to be put in a psychiatric hospital for care. If you are a danger to yourself and others, it becomes necessary to have you admitted for around-the-clock care.

3. Brain-Stimulus treatment

Some mental illnesses can be stubborn or the person suffering from them is so stubborn that medications and even psychotherapy do not work. These conditions that are determined to make their home and protect it at all costs are dealt with using brain stimuli. The patient may undergo electroconvulsive therapy, deep brain stimulation, vagus nerve stimulation or repetitive transcranial magnetic stimulation.

4. Substance-Abuse treatment

As mentioned earlier, some of the mental illnesses stem from the abuse of alcohol and drugs. In other cases, the mental disorder can push someone to start abusing drugs in a bid to deal with the symptoms. At times, you can find someone with a social disorder taking a shot or two of tequila to calm his nerves down. Over time, this becomes a norm and, since the anxiety is always there when has to go for social events, he quickly becomes addicted. Even for those on other treatment methods, the intake of alcohol and drugs interferes with their success. Specialized treatment for substance abuse is therefore offered to the patient.

5. Psychotherapy

In psychotherapy sessions, you talk to a mental-health professional about your condition and learn more about it. Some people call it **Talk Therapy** or collaborative treatment. With this understanding and the insights gained, it becomes easy to learn about coping strategies and skills to manage stress. Besides, since the sessions take a few months, it provides time to adjust. In some cases, there is a need for long-term treatment. The good thing with psychotherapy is that you can have sessions in groups to learn from others or even include your support people, like family.

There are different psychotherapy treatment plans that you can choose from that are Empirically Supported Treatments (ESTs) are:

- ***Psychodynamic Psychotherapy*** focuses on improving awareness of unconscious behaviors and thoughts, conflict resolution, and the development of new insights into various motivations.
- ***Supportive Psychotherapy*** emphasizes your coping abilities with stress and other difficult situations.
- ***Cognitive Behavioral Therapy (CBT)*** helps in the identification of unhealthy negative behaviors and beliefs and helps to replace these with positive and healthy ones.

<u>In this book, we will focus on Cognitive Behavioral Therapy, one of the most effective treatment plans for depression and anxiety, as well as intuitive thoughts.</u>

CBT boasts as the most effective psychological method of treating both moderate and severe depression.

Having personally gone through CBT for intrusive thoughts and depression, I can confidently endorse this method as having great success. Besides, you have the option of having a support system to walk through the journey with you. CBT provides simple techniques that you can practice with ease to get good results.

What is Cognitive Behavioral Therapy?

CBT is one of the psychotherapeutic treatments that helps you identify disturbing, destructive and undesired thought patterns that negatively influence emotions and behavior. When you know what ails you, it is now possible to change these patterns and develop positive behavior and emotions.

Over the years, CBT has been extensively used in the treatment of most mental illnesses, including anxiety, depression, eating disorders, severe mental disorders, as well as problems associated with alcohol and drug use. Evidence from research studies show that CBT is more effective than psychiatric medications or other kinds of psychological therapy. CBT can even help in the management of marital problems. You don't have to trust me; just try it for yourself. Additionally, engaging in Cognitive Behavioral Therapy has a way of improving the functioning and quality of your life. You do not only get psychologically well but also live a great and fulfilling life, all thanks to CBT.

You can relax in the knowledge that the advances made in CBT over the years have been based on both clinical practice and research. There is no trial and error. In addition to having successfully gone through the process and seen positive results, there is much scientific evidence to show that this form of therapy produces positive change.

Core principles of CBT

Some of the most important principles that form the basis for CBT include:

- Unhelpful or faulty ways of thinking form the foundation for psychological problems.
- Unhelpful behavior or learned patterns also form the basis of psychological problems.
- Those affected by psychological problems can learn better coping strategies that help to relieve their symptoms and help them to live more effective lives.

CBT employs different strategies in an effort to change thinking patterns, such as:

- Learning to identify the distortions in your thinking that are causing problems and then re-looking at them from a reality point of view.
- Developing a clearer understanding of the behavior, as well as the behavior of others.
- Learning to use problem-solving skills when faced with a difficult situation.
- Gaining greater self-confidence in your abilities.

When working on a change in behavioral patterns, some CBT strategies that are helpful include:

- Instead of avoiding or running away from your fears, you face them head on.
- Preparation is key. You can prepare for those difficult and problematic interactions with others by role-playing so you can boost your confidence in handling similar situations.
- Learning to relax the body and calm the mind down so you do not overreact and behave in an inappropriate manner.

Unlike other modes of treatment, CBT allows you and the psychologist to work together collaboratively to clearly understand the problem and come up with a workable treatment strategy. In a way, you learn to be your own therapist through the exercises you engage in during sessions as well as the take-home work that you do. Unlike medication that is reliant on an external source of help, CBT helps you to look within you to find the answers that you need and draw the necessary strength to carry forward.

Ultimately, CBT is based on your current life. Some of the challenges you are facing may be drawn from your past, and it is important to acknowledge that part of your life. However, CBT does not give much emphasis on the past but rather the present. The target here is to ensure that you move forward in life by developing effective ways of coping.

Some of the Common Mental Disorders

Anxiety Disorders

If you experience distressing and frequent apprehension and fear, you are likely to be suffering from an anxiety disorder. We all feel anxious from time to time especially in stressful situations. However, when you have an anxiety disorder, you tend to feel so even during non-stressful situations. The bouts may go for long periods of time, sometimes even half a year at a time.

The term 'anxiety disorders' refers to a number of conditions, including:

Obsessive Compulsive Disorder (OCD)

OCD is a mental condition that causes a person to have repeated unwanted sensations or thoughts (obsessions). The person may also have the urge to keep doing something over and over (compulsions). For example, a person can have an obsessive thought that some numbers are bad or have the compulsion to check the locks about three times each night or wash their hands five times after touching anything dirty. Although we all have certain habits that we keep repeating, having OCD means that these actions and thoughts are not enjoyable, take up more than an hour every day, are beyond one's control, and interfere with life, be it the work or social part of it. The four general categories of OCD include:

- *Contamination*: You fear possibly dirty things and have a compulsion to clean. You may also experience mental contamination where you feel like you are being treated like dirt.

- *Checking*: Repeated checking of locks, switches, systems or even medical conditions or pregnancy. Picture someone who conducts a pregnancy test every few days because they think they may be pregnant.
- *Intrusive thoughts and ruminations*: Here, you become obsessed with a particular line of thought, and some thoughts are disturbing or violent.
- *Symmetry and order*: You want all things lined up in a certain way. Some people go as far as arranging their cereals according to color.

Post-Traumatic Stress Disorder (PTSD)

When you have been through a terrifying event, like war or a fire, there is the possibility of developing a mental-health condition. The common symptoms include nightmares, flashbacks, uncontrollable thoughts about the traumatic event and severe anxiety.

Anyone who goes through a traumatic event will have difficulty coping and adjusting to life, but over time and with good care, it is possible to get better. In some cases, the trauma is so much that the symptoms keep getting worse and can last for months or years, making it difficult to live a full life. When the traumatic event hinders you from functioning normally, you may have Post-Traumatic Stress Disorder.

Panic Disorder

You may have panic disorder if you experience recurring but unanticipated panic attacks. Panic is the intense discomfort or fear that rises to a peak within minutes. The problem with panic disorder is that the people suffering from it tend to live in fear of having an attack, which makes them tense and consequently increases their chance of having one. Visualize a situation where you fear failure so much that you live in fear of failing only to end up failing. That sounds more complicated than it is.

Symptoms of panic disorder include sweating, breathing difficulties and a racing heart. In essence, you feel like the world is falling apart without any warning, suffocating or choking.

Social Anxiety Disorder

Have you ever had butterflies on a first date? Or felt them flapping their wings just before you start an important presentation? You have nothing to worry about; that is part of life, but not for everyone. Some people suffer from social phobia also called social anxiety disorder. For them, everyday interactions are a cause of significant anxiety, embarrassment, self-consciousness and fear. They are afraid of being judged or scrutinized by others and opt to avoid others as much as possible leading to a disruption in their daily activities.

People with social phobia worry about embarrassing themselves and that others will notice their anxiety. They will therefore avoid being the center of attention, avoid speaking for fear of embarrassment, and even get anxious at the thought of meeting others or being in a socially involved event. Physical symptoms include trembling, sweating, blushing, muscle tension, dizziness, nausea and trouble catching their breath. If you experience social phobia, you may find your mind going blank when someone asks you even a simple question.

Generalized Anxiety Disorder (GAD)

Having GAD means that you have an uncontrollable worry about common situations and occurrences. Some people refer to it as chronic anxiety neurosis. Often, we worry about one thing or another, particularly finances, but if you have GAD, you will worry several times daily for many months even when there is nothing to worry about. Sometimes you may not even know what you are worrying about except feeling that something bad may happen. At this point, the worry takes over your life, and it affects your daily activities and relationships with others.

Symptoms of GAD include sleep problems, poor concentration, irritability, shaking, rapid heartbeat, sweaty palms, muscle tension and even diarrhoea. All that worrying can be tiresome, resulting in fatigue and exhaustion.

You are likely to get GAD if you have family members with anxiety, faced abuse in childhood, take excessive caffeine or tobacco that escalates existing anxiety, and are exposed to stressful situations for a long time.

Mood Disorders

There is a saying that says, "Not every day is Sunday", meaning that days vary, and each day brings with it different tidings. We all experience mood swings. At least one in every 10 adults suffers from a type of mood disorder that disrupts their lives. If you are among them, you will have severe and persistent symptoms that make life difficult. The symptoms vary as per the specific disorder, but generally they include excessive guilt, feeling hopeless, low self-esteem and reduced energy.

Psychotic Disorders

People suffering from psychotic disorders lose their sense of reality such that they can't tell what is real and what is not. Some contributing factors to this disorder include certain viruses' trauma, extreme stress, drug abuse, and the working (or lack of working) of specific brain circuits.

Eating Disorders

There is more to food than meets the mouth. How you relate to food has a lot to do with your mental state. You may have noticed that many of the mental disorders tend to affect a person's relationship with food, either through overeating or not eating. Eating disorders can be manifested through an obsession with body weight, shape or food. For some people, the situation is so bad that they end up dead if the condition is not treated. Symptoms include food binges, severe food restriction, over-exercising or purging behaviors.

That is not all

There are many other mental illnesses, including different types of phobias and personality disorders. Some common and 'normal' emotions, like anger and loneliness, can easily turn into mental illnesses when they get out of hand and harm you or others. For instance, my father had anger issues that saw the death of my mother. In my anger, also, I wrecked my family, depriving them and myself of peace. At this point anger is no longer a natural emotion, but a mental problem that needs to be addressed.

Other behaviors, like hoarding, are not necessarily mental problems until they go to the extreme. They may also indicate the existence of another mental disorder.

CHAPTER TWO

Safety Plan

When you are going through a mental illness, life can be tough and quite unbearable. Most days seem endless and full of pressure, while you lack the energy and the will to go through it. With negative thoughts and emotions weighing you down, it is expected that your behavior will align with how you feel and think. The result is guilt for behaving badly, hopelessness and a lack of motivation to get up.

I remember that Wednesday morning as I sat in my well-furnished executive office feeling empty and beaten. Despite the wealth and success, I felt like a failure and lost beyond redemption. At times like those, destructive thoughts creep in. You begin to feel that leaving this world is the only way to fill that hole within, quiet the constant buzz in the mind, and be accepted. While deadly thoughts keep showing up now and then, there are days when the cry for peace and quiet is so loud that it takes a lot of willpower to stop it. Without a safety plan, it is easy to answer this call and take the short and foolish route out. I know, I attempted it. I took those pills.

Since you are aware of the existence of such extra gloomy days, it is best to plan for them, and that is where the safety plan comes in. Diagnosis of a mental illness is not enough to keep you and others from harm. The safety plan will help you identify your red flags. You will know when you have started going downhill, and even the rate of acceleration, so you can seek the necessary help.

Even if you are not yet suicidal, as long as you have a mental disorder, it is best to have a safety plan. That way, you stay prepared in case things get out of hand. Knowing what to do takes away one more cause for anxiety.

Before you prepare your safety plan, you need to be at a good place. You can hardly think through your triggers when you are on the verge of self-harm. An appropriate time to prepare the plan is when you are recovering or stable. Have with you a mental-health provider and a family member or one of your support people. In case you are unable to realize the red flags, he can help you. Having someone to support you is also crucial, so you don't feel alone.

If you're wondering how having a safety plan helps your life, you can look at recent studies that show that it is an evidence-based intervention that reduces the risk of harming yourself or others. Patients who have a safety plan are less likely to self-harm than those without. Additionally, they tend to have subsequently better-quality engagements with the health-care providers. You should be part of the winning team, and a small step to take is the development of a safety plan.

The safety plan is your first aid kit to help you through a crisis and ensure that you stay safe before pulling the big guns, if necessary. It affords you time to calm down and feel more in control when those overwhelming thoughts come.

What to consider when developing a plan

When developing a safety plan, there are certain issues you need to consider to ensure that your plan works. You will realize that these vary from one individual to another, making it important for each person to develop a safety plan that is tailored to himself. Some of the questions you need to ask yourself include:

1. *When to use the plan:* You need to ask yourself at what point you need to use the plan. At this point, it is necessary to consider what triggers the deadly thoughts. Look at the possible situations, feelings or thoughts, and any warning signs that you can recognize. For example, if

you stop eating when you're feeling depressed, then you know that is a sign to watch for.

2. ***How to comfort yourself:*** Similar to the above where you create a list of what sets you off on the dangerous path, here you also create a similar list but of those things that make you feel better so you can reduce the destructive thoughts. You need to look at things that make you feel protected and safe. For example, there are those who clean, or those for which food is the answer. For you, it might be taking a walk or listening to music. Whatever works for you, even if it is shouting or jumping up and down, do not hesitate to write it down.

3. ***Reasons for living:*** There are days so dark that you may not see any reason for being alive. All you want to do is disappear into thin air and never feel pained or weighed down again. Before you get to that day, write down your reasons for living so that you remember why life is worth living. Your reasons could be anything like family, a pet, partner or anything else. There is no need to justify any of the reasons you choose. Even your potted plants, if they give you the joy and reason to live, then that's

all that matters. You only need something or someone that makes life worth living.

4. ***Who to talk to:*** In our darkest hours, there are not many numbers on our phones that are worth dialing. In most cases, you hardly feel like talking to anyone. However, it is necessary that you find one or two people who you can talk to in those times. These are people who are not judgmental and who truly understand your situation and are willing to take the time to help you feel better. You can even ask them if you can add them to your list of people who you would reach out to when feeling down and having dangerous thoughts. Again, include people you feel comfortable talking to, like a friend, partner or even a priest.

5. ***Where to get professional help:*** In as much as it is important to have people around you, it is also important to have a list of available and easily accessible professional help that can provide you with any support that you may need. The list can include mental-health professionals and helplines, email addresses and website addresses that you can reach out to.

6. ***How to make your environment safe:*** Sometimes all it takes is the presence of a potential weapon to push one over the edge. Therefore, you have to make a conscious decision to ensure that your environment is safe for you. You may need to secure items that you could use to harm yourself or even get out of an unsafe environment. You could also ask someone else to help you stay safe. For example, if you are likely to hurt yourself in the kitchen, it is best to get out of there. Alternatively, you may want to lock up any sharp items, like knives and pairs of scissors. Highly lethal methods or items, like firearms and poison, should not be left for the patient to restrict. A designated and responsible person, like a close friend, police or even a family member, should be charged with the responsibility of making these restrictions.

The questions above make up your safety plan. You need to document the answers and keep them in an easily accessible place for reference when you need them. The safety plan is best prepared with the input of a mental-health professional, as well as someone who you trust. You need all the help you can get, and it is always nice to have a team to discuss issues with, lest those issues overwhelm you. As you may have noted, making a safety plan is not rocket science, so you have nothing to worry about. The bulk of the work remains in ensuring that it is implemented.

What happens after developing the plan?

Alongside your mental-health-care team of professionals, it is important that you discuss the likelihood that the safety plan will be followed when the need arises. There is no need for taking time to develop a safety plan only for it to be discarded at the first sign of trouble. If you see any possible hindrances to the implementation of the safety plan, then this is a good time to disclose them for further discussion. Together, these concerns can be addressed to ensure that, when or if the time comes, you will follow the plan.

The safety plan has to be easily accessible to you at all times. After its development, it is also crucial that you discuss where you keep the plan, so it is safe yet easily accessible. You can have both a hard and soft copy that are placed in strategic places for your reference.

Another important factor is to evaluate if the format used for the plan is appropriate and fits within your capacity and circumstances. The idea is to keep the safety plan as simple as possible to avoid contradictions or any complicated phrases.

Finally, you have to keep reviewing the plan periodically to ensure that it is still effective. Over time, your circumstances are likely to change, and the plan needs to reflect this change. For example, if the person you reach out to when feeling overwhelmed moves to a different place and a different time zone, you may want to have someone else take their place and who can easily read you and the medical assistance that you need.

You need to note that sometimes having the safety plan is not enough to deter the dangerous feelings. If the feelings persist despite doing what your plan intends that you do, then it is time to ask for assistance from the nearest emergency room. Do not wait for tomorrow, and do not take yourself to the hospital. Instead, call the emergency services team for your area and request for transport to the hospital.

Implementing the Safety Plan

Now that you have a plan at hand, the next time you have such thoughts or signs of triggers that you recognize as red signs, take out your plan and follow the outlined course of action until you feel safe again. For example, if you are feeling unnaturally angry or very low, you can take a walk or use whatever way of calming yourself down that is in your plan until you feel better. However, if the feelings are very strong, you can simply call a trusted friend or emergency services who can come stay with you. If you can, take action at the onset of the thoughts or even when you recognize any red flags, so you are able to calm down sooner rather than later.

The safety plan is meant to be your support and, if, at any point, you feel overwhelmed, do not consider yourself a loser but be the champion by calling in emergency services. Remember, above all else, your life is most important.

Chapter Summary

Having a safety plan is a crucial step in the management of any mental illness.

- You have to know and recognize your triggers.
- Get a good support team.
- Be willing to follow the safety plan.
- Keep the plan updated as your recovery/illness progresses.

In the next chapter, you will learn about the first CBT technique that you can use to overcome anxiety, depression and intrusive thoughts: a technique called cognitive restructuring.

CHAPTER THREE

Technique 1– Cognitive Restructuring

If we were all to be truthful, we would say that we have some days that are better than others. We all experience negative thoughts once in a while, but for some people, these thoughts become entrenched into them, almost becoming a part of them and thus interfering with their well-being, achievements and relationships. When you are in such a position, it becomes hard to think clearly and even more difficult to get those thoughts from your mind. You may be feeling beaten, but you are not done yet. The overwhelming and burdening thoughts that you have may seem to be taking center stage in your life, but there is a way of changing those thoughts.

What is Cognitive Restructuring?

Cognitive restructuring is a Cognitive Behavioral Therapy (CBT) technique, which helps you to notice as well as change those negative thinking patterns. Through cognitive restructuring, you can find ways to explore, interrupt and redirect self-defeating and destructive thoughts. The cognitive restructuring technique is known as a useful tool that can help you get a good understanding of those unhappy feelings, as well as for challenging the 'automatic beliefs' that are often wrong.

When beginning to use cognitive reconstructing, it is advisable to work with a therapist to help you overcome the hurdle of recognizing those faulty thought patterns that have made a home in your mind. Most times, you are so used to thinking in a particular way that it becomes very difficult to find those inaccuracies in your thought patterns that are causing you problems.

Cognitive restructuring has its foundation on cognitive mediation, which implies that your emotional feelings are not based on what happens to you but rather how you process and think about what happens to you. Here, it is literally the thought that counts. If you change how you think, you can also change how you feel.

Application and Success

Before we delve into how to carry out cognitive restructuring, you may want to know if it works or is a waste of time. Having been through the process, I can attest that this technique produces positive results. Over time, I have been able to successfully change those negative thinking patterns to positive ones, and I have seen my behavior and state of mind change for the better.

There are also many research studies that have shown that cognitive restructuring is an effective technique in the treatment of different conditions, such as depression, social phobias, PTSD, stress, anxiety, addictions and relationship issues. Furthermore, this technique has been proven to help people dealing with extreme grief.

You can easily apply cognitive restructuring into your everyday life when faced with those negative thoughts. However, do not pass up a chance to work through the process with a mental-health practitioner to ensure a higher chance of success.

Steps in Cognitive Restructuring

The cognitive restructuring framework is based on the Seven-Column Thought Record, designed by Christine Padesky, and takes you through below simple steps.

- ***Calm down:*** Looking within yourself while stressed or upset is very difficult. The first step is to ensure that you are calm. You can take some time to engage in deep breathing or the use of meditation to calm yourself. Once calm, you can then begin the process and be able to deal with any intrusive thoughts.

- ***Situation identification:*** The next step is to identify the situation you are in and what is triggering the negative mood. For example, is it something someone said to you? Was it a situation you walked into? The more specific you can be in this situation, the better. For instance, if you submit a report and someone makes a remark that sends you flying off the handle, think through the comment and pick out what exactly in that comment has destabilized your emotions.

- ***Carry out mood analysis:*** Once you put a finger on the situation, you also need to analyze your mood through it. The key thing here is to focus and isolate the mood, while leaving out the thoughts. The easiest way to separate the two is to recognize that a thought tends to be complex. For example, "He hated my report for including recommendations that he did not like." Moods are often easy to relate to and can be summarized in one word. For example, the incident resulted in humiliation, anger, sadness, frustration or insecurity.

- ***Identify automatic thoughts:*** Next, you need to write down the automatic thoughts or the natural reactions that you experience when you feel the mood. For example, you may think you are stupid or that he is arrogant, or that you will never get that promotion, or that you were right. Whatever thought automatically crops into your mind after the mood kicks in, you need to write it down.

- ***Find objectively supporting evidence:*** On this part, calmly and rationally look at a reason that supports why you are having those automatic thoughts. For example, the boss did not consider even one of my recommendations or even ask why I thought they were ideal." Here, your goal is to be as objective as possible while looking at the scenario, then write down the specific comment or event that caused you to have those automatic thoughts.

- ***Find objectively contradicting evidence:*** Similar to the above, here you also look at the scenario objectively then identify and note down anything that evidently contradicts that automatic thought. For example, "Those recommendations were based on research findings." You can also look at your record and note that you have always produced quality reports and that you train new people on producing ideal reports. By looking at this and writing them down, you realize that these statements are fair and a true reflection of your position, as compared to the reactive thoughts.

- ***Identify the thoughts that are fair and balanced:*** By now, you have carefully analyzed the situation and thought through your reactions. You have the necessary information to identify a fair and balanced perspective of the occurrences. However, you may still feel uncertain, so you can discuss the situation with another person or use another way to test the question. You can now write down the balanced thoughts. For example, you can note that your report contained the right information based on facts, and his way of handling the situation was not appropriate. Or you can write that, "I did my best on that report, and it was great except the recommendations that the boss did not like." Do not look to justify yourself but to describe the situation as it is. If you realize there were errors on the report, acknowledge them but do not center on them. You can write that the report was wonderfully done but had a possibly misleading recommendation that did not alter the tone or the effectiveness of it.

- *Monitor your mood:* Once you have calmly gone through the situation, you will realize that having a clear view makes you feel better. You are likely to be in a better mood feeling positive. Write down how you feel.

- *Reflect:* Since you are already feeling better, it is a good time to reflect on what you can do about the situation. You may realize after writing down the fair and balanced view that you need not take any action and that it is not a big deal as you originally envisioned it. However, if you feel like there is something you can do, then go ahead. For example, if, after the comment, you got angry and banged the doors, you may want to go and apologize for that.

- *Create positive affirmations:* There is power in our words. By making affirmations, you remind yourself of all the capabilities that you have and convince yourself to embrace positivity. These positive utterances become part of you and will help to keep away any negative automatic thoughts in future.

The Challenge

The only challenge is that cognitive restructuring is not very easy to learn for some people. To put it into perspective, it is not difficult to learn either, but some people find identifying their moods and feelings and putting them into words to be difficult. Also, in the event that you make any thought errors, it is difficult to recognize them. Additionally, you may have trouble restating your thoughts in a way that does not make more thought errors.

The good news is that it is not all bleak. With patience, practice, and an open mind you can master cognitive restructuring. A helpful tactic is to have a third-party present during the process, preferably a therapist, who is able to critique your efforts while coaching you to succeed.

Why you should try Cognitive Restructuring

In addition to the high potential for success that comes with this technique, look at it as a type of mental weightlifting. The first time it is going to be challenging, and your muscles will ache just like what happens at the gym. However, you do not give up in those first days even as it seems extremely tough because your mental muscles are developing and strengthening. As you continually practice, it will get easier, and your mental muscles will gain strength. You will be surprised that, with time, they are so strong that you easily catch yourself when you start to have dysfunctional thinking and are able to correct the thought in real time, so you don't experience stress. Wouldn't you want that?

Today, I do not even consciously tell myself that I will undertake cognitive restructuring, it has become embedded in me and occurs almost automatically. Each time a negative and stress-inducing thought crops into my head, I am alert, and I calmly ask myself what caused it and correct my thought process. You can also experience the liberation that comes with not having to feel useless and weighed down.

Chapter Summary

In this chapter, we have looked at one CBT technique to address some of the major mental illnesses, including depression, anxiety and intrusive thoughts. We have learned that:

- Cognitive restructuring is a technique that focuses on identifying, challenging and altering the negative thoughts and making way for positive thoughts.
- Through this technique, you will learn to replace those rigid and hard-on-yourself thoughts with less rigid, more accurate and practical thoughts that align you to think positively.
- Although, initially the technique may be challenging, especially when it comes to being true to yourself and your thoughts, it gets better, easier and more effective as time goes on.
- Practice makes perfect.

In the next chapter, you will learn about another CBT technique on bursting mental distortions.

CHAPTER FOUR

Technique 2 – Bursting Mental Distortions

There are days when you wake up and feel like you are full of negativity. Some people believe that the day will be bad even before their feet touch the floor while others do not even have the will to get out of bed. The feeling is usually brought about something that your mind was focused on or a worry within you. True, we all do experience those negative feelings brought about by the negative thoughts we harbor.

You are not alone. Even those among us who take pride in being balanced thinkers are plagued with these negative thoughts from time to time. The difference is that they know when to burst such a thought and not allow it to grow roots. Psychologists call these inaccurate thoughts, which only work to reinforce negative emotions or thought patterns, cognitive distortions that make us interpret events in a negative light. Having cognitive distortions from time to time is normal. However, when they are reinforced, they deepen depression, increase anxiety, cause difficulties in relationships and result in other major complications.

Cognitive Distortions

You may wonder where these cognitive distortions come from and how best to deal with them. Evidence from research shows that people develop them as a means of coping with life's adverse events. The more severe and prolonged those events are, the stronger and more likely the cognitive distortions will be. Stress causes people to adapt their way of thinking in a way that is useful for their immediate survival. For example, if every time it gets dark it rains, people learn to prepare for rain at the first sight of darkness. Similarly, our early ancestors used cognitive distortions to adapt to the changing environment. However, as you may know, life is not constant and, while on a dark day it may rain, it is not given that every dark day brings rain with it. Therefore, constantly giving in to cognitive distortions results in habitual errors in thinking.

Let us look at some of the most common cognitive distortions that you are likely to be encouraging in your life. Sometimes we do not realize that we allow our thinking to be flawed by some of these distortions. More often than not, you may not even recognize them for what they are.

- ***Polarized Thinking:*** You can consider this to be 'all or nothing thinking.' Everything is either black or white without any room for gray or even the addition of color. It is either you are extremely good or a failure, and there is no middle ground. For example, you may think that you are a total failure if you do not play the piano well, even if you have just started playing. You're not recognizing that you are not skilled (yet) and need time to learn.

- *Filtering:* In this cognitive distortion, you may find that you ignore all the good and positive and instead focus all your attention and thoughts on the negative aspect albeit however small it may be. For example, if you invite people over for dinner and everyone comes except for one person, you spend the evening focused on why he didn't come and allowing negative thoughts to cloud your mind instead of enjoying dinner with the company that is attending.

- *Jumping to conclusions:* Here, you find yourself drawing conclusions and being sure of something even without any evidence. For example, you may conclude that the one person who did not attend your dinner does not like you and that the one who did attend only came to mock you. Also, you may find yourself believing that whatever fears you have will come true even before you have the chance to find out.

- ***Overgeneralization:*** We all tend to overgeneralize from time to time. Overgeneralization involves taking a single and isolated incident and drawing broad conclusions from it. For example, if you fail one job interview, you may conclude that you are terrible at interviews and may never get a job.

- ***Personalization:*** There are people who carry the weight of the world on their shoulders simply by personalizing matters. They feel like their actions impact other people or external events and, hence, hold themselves responsible. For example, they may feel like by buying the last container of milk at the store they are the reason it has run out and others will not have any.

- ***Magnifying, Minimizing or Catastrophizing:*** There are two sides to this: either minimizing the positives or magnifying the negatives. In this distortion, the person may take a small mistake made and catastrophize it. For example, if she is late for a meeting, she may think that the entire project will run late because of it and worry about being fired for derailing the project. On the other hand, she may play down any accomplishment she achieves and reduce herself to mere invisibility.

- ***Control fallacies:*** Some of us like being in control of everything and that everything that happens to us is either out of our own actions or purely external forces. People with control fallacies have a hard time accepting that sometimes things happen from forces that we can't control. For example, a person with this cognitive distortion will assume that other people's performances are not good because of them, or theirs is not good because of a difficult co-worker.

- ***Blaming:*** Most often, when things go wrong, we have to find a way of explaining the outcome. Some people opt to blame others for making them feel or act in a certain manner, which is a cognitive distortion. No matter how someone contributes to the situation, the only person solely responsible for how you act or feel is you.

- ***Fairness fallacies:*** As a matter of fact, life is not fair. However, there are people who go through life so fixated on fairness that they end up unhappy and resentful when they do not get it.

- ***Emotional reasoning:*** If you are one of those people who has a strong false belief in your emotions, then that is a cognitive distortion. The way you feel about a situation cannot be necessarily true and, hence, is not a definite or accurate indicator of reality. Listening to, validating and expressing emotions is important, but you should judge things based on reality and rational evidence.

- ***Labeling:*** There are people who reduce themselves or others to a single, mainly negative, descriptor or characteristic, such as a failure or being stupid. Labeling causes people to criticize themselves and also causes the thinker to either underestimate or misunderstand others due to the misperception.

- ***Positive discounting:*** Similar to filtering, people who discount the positive have a negative bias in their thinking. They tend to explain any positive away as a fluke or luck instead of acknowledging that good things do occur as a result of skills, determination and smart choices.

- ***The 'should' people:*** Have you met one of those people who always has a list of what should be done or said in a certain situation? He should be able to do this when that happens. His thinking is limited to this and will usually have a negative perspective of life. Most of these kinds of people are rooted in internalized cultural or family expectations that are not appropriate as they tend to increase anxiety and reduce self-esteem.

How to Burst Cognitive Distortions

In this section, we look at what you can do to fix those irrational and automatic thoughts, as well as cognitive distortions.

- ***Identify it:*** The first step is to identify the kind of distortion that you are harboring and its extent in your life. This is similar to when you get sick and the doctor examines you to determine the problem and, thus, the solution. You can only work to change what you know to be the problem. Start by tracking your thoughts daily and identifying any cognitive distortions. A simple way of doing this is by developing a list of troublesome thoughts as they keep coming, then you can comb through them and see if they match up with any cognitive distortions. Taking time to go through your negative and intrusive thoughts at a later time helps you to realize what cognitive distortion(s) you are leaning toward. You can also take this opportunity to carefully look into each problem in a calm, realistic and natural manner. Consider it as keeping a mood log.

- ***Examine the evidence:*** Here, you need to distance yourself from the emotionality of the upsetting episode or event, then take the judge's seat to examine the evidence objectively. You will be able to identify the basis for your distorted view. You can easily achieve this by looking at individual thoughts linked to an event, and then objectively deciding whether they are a reflection of either a fact or an opinion. For example, thoughts such as, "I am stupid" or "I am selfish" are opinions. On the other hand, statements like, "My boss spoke to me angrily" or "I submitted the report late" are facts. You need to separate the facts and opinions so you can determine which is a cognitive distortion, then you can work on that.

- ***Apply the double-standard method:*** As an alternative to the negative, demeaning and harsh self-talk that you keep telling yourself, consider turning this negative talk into a caring and compassionate one, such as one you would give a friend. Most people with mental illnesses tend to be very hard on themselves while being more accommodating to friends and relatives. You should take the time to go through your thoughts and situation, look at yourself as a close friend and have a similar conversation as you would have with her, heck, even make that important cup of tea, and converse. Would you tell your friends after working hard on a report that she was going to screw up, and it wasn't any good? Chances are high that you would tell them not to worry because they did give it their best and that the report was going to be exceptionally well-received. Tell yourself the same thing, be your own friend. Besides, in a world with few friends, it helps to have one within.

- ***Welcome the shades of gray:*** When you are carrying different cognitive distortions, your mind tends to simplify the processing of stimuli and will often rush to make a decision or choose a response. Although black and white thinking or polarized thinking do serve a good purpose of hastening decision-making and responses, it can also take you on a road of irrational belief. You need to welcome the shades of gray and stop focusing on either black or white. When the plan did not fully succeed, don't look at it as having failed but instead evaluate it on a scale of 0 and 100. That way, you get to appreciate the amount that is achieved, and also understand how much is remaining and why. For example, if you have been working hard at something then get so tired you take a day off, don't think the effort of the days worked is wasted because of that one day. If you decide to work out and have been doing so for weeks, then one day you don't work out and have that cake, don't give up because you think you are a failure. Look at the scale and appreciate how much you have gotten done, then analyze and see that the one day of being easy on yourself could be beneficial to re-energize you. The overall likelihood of ruining everything could be around two percent, a very negligible number.

- ***Experiment:*** Another way of bursting cognitive distortions is to experiment, much like scientists do when trying to prove a hypothesis. The idea here is to look for evidence that those thoughts you are having are true. For example, if you have been thinking that you are unable to do a certain task and so, as a result, you have neglected to even attempt it. You could test that perceived inability by breaking the task into small sub-tasks and attempting to do just one or two. You may be surprised that you can make a lot of progress and that will prove that your thought on it was a cognitive distortion. For example, if you have been telling yourself that you are not good enough and cannot pass that class, start by registering for it and attending the first class with an open mind. You may realize that you enjoy the content and end up doing really well. Take time to test those thoughts; do not allow them to intimidate you. If you think your friends hate you, ask them to dinner, and you may be surprised to see how glad they are that you reached out. Develop a policy that says that it is not true until proven so. You will note that the cognitive distortions will begin to disappear as they know they are bound to be proven wrong.

- ***Take a survey:*** When you feel weighed down, in doubt and filled with negative intrusive thoughts, it helps to talk to someone. They say a problem shared is half-solved. In this case, go a little further and ask people their opinions on the reality of your attitude and thoughts. Preferably, ask people who are in a similar situation to yours. For example, if you are working hard on your body through exercise and eating healthy and believe that falling into the temptation of a cheat meal is unforgivable, you can ask your gym instructor or that well-toned girl. They will tell you that cheating on your meals happens every so often, and it is nothing to fret over as long as you don't make it a habit. You can even double-check by asking the same question to a few more people to hear their experiences.

- ***Watch the semantics:*** If you are one of the people stuck in the world of 'should' or 'should not', it is time to get out of it. Using 'should' statements applies unwritten rules to how you can behave, which is something that may not make any sense to others. 'Should' statements imply that you are judging your behavior or that of another person, which is hurtful and unnecessary. When you catch yourself starting to make a should statement, try something else like, "It would be good or nice if…". That creates a more positive feel. For instance, you could say, "It would be nice if I started exercising for better health." The positivity of the statement first gives you a choice, hence, making you feel in control and increasing your chances of taking up exercise. At the same time, if, for some reason, you cannot exercise, maybe due to health concerns, it still gives you a way out without feeling like a failure. In a similar situation, if you use should, you end up feeling as though you ought to and if you don't or cannot for whatever reason, you have failed, which is not true. You can take back control by simply changing your semantics.

- ***Look up the definition:*** Yes, I mean get a dictionary or go to the Internet and search the meaning of those labels that you are giving to yourself and others. This method works better for the intellectual people who like to argue on the basis of facts, but can work with anyone who is willing to look up the meaning of words and phrases. Once you are armed with information, you can argue against your cognitive distortions. If you have labeled yourself as stupid or inferior, looking at the meaning of the words will instantly tell you that these labels do not refer to a person in his entirety but rather to specific behaviors. You can then go on to ask further questions like, "Stupid in what? Have I been taught or trained? For how long? How much do I know? Stupid compared to who? How much does the other person know? What level of education and experience does he have?" As you think about the definitions, you delve further into questioning your reasoning and realize that such labels are not true and are a waste of your brain power.

- ***Re-attributions:*** Some of us suffer from blaming and from personalized cognitive disorders, meaning that they point at themselves and take the fall for every negative thing that they experience. They believe that they are synonymous with causing bad things. If you are one of these people, you do not look at the actual cause but rather convince yourself that it is because of you. Re-attribution helps you to identify external factors or people that contribute to the event or problem, so you stop blaming yourself. By assigning responsibility where it is due, you are not deflecting blame but rather showing the true contributors and not placing the entire blame on you. You will then have the energy not to feel bad for causing something you did not cause, but to pursue resolutions to the problems and find ways of dealing with the predicaments. For example, if you are a six-person team working on a research project, and the work is not done in due time due to adverse weather that prevents field work from going on as planned, you cannot blame yourself for the delay. You have to acknowledge the role of nature and then split the responsibility among the six of you, making it ⅙th your responsibility. Instead of wallowing in guilt for missed deadlines, you should be working to find a way to fast-track the remaining work.

- ***Weigh the costs and the benefits:*** In this method of bursting cognitive distortions, you rely on motivation rather than facts. Here, you list the pros and cons of thoughts, feelings and behaviors that you are experiencing. You can, therefore, figure out what you are gaining by having that distorted thinking, feeling bad and behavior that is inappropriate. You will have to look within and ask yourself how believing and holding on to the situations and negative thinking helps you. If, after listing the pros and cons, you find that the cons outweigh the pros, then you are better off without the distortions and irrational thinking. You have the weapon to talk back those ugly thoughts and welcome the positive ones.

How to Stop or Slow Down Cognitive Distortions

Now that you know how to burst those cognitive distortions, it is also important to know how to slow down or stop those distortions when they creep up. In addition to finding the right way to unravel those distortions, here is a simple way of stopping them, or at least slowing them down, when they occur.

- ***Identify and isolate that intrusive or negative thought:*** Examine your thoughts well and recognize some words that are clues to cognitive distortions, such as 'never', 'always' or 'can't'. Other strong and negative words, such as loser, foolish or hate should also give you clues into cognitive distortions.

- ***Write it down:*** By now, you may realize the importance of writing things down. Writing down those thoughts make them come alive so you can assess them easily.

- ***Check your distress temperature:*** On a scale of 0 to 10, with zero being peaceful and content and 10 being the feeling of the whole world ending, check where you fall on that scale.

- ***Is it reasonable?*** The next question to ask is if the thought you are having is reasonable. Be very honest with yourself and answer if you think your thinking pattern makes sense. An easy way of doing so is saying the thought out loud. For example, "I am stupid." Assume a friend or colleague said that to you. Would you agree? If you find that the thought you are having is reasonable, there is a likelihood that it is not a cognitive distortion. For instance, if you think you are lazy and you find that it is true, then take stock of what caused the thought, then decide to do something about it, or let go or even let go of the thought but work on the cause. There is always much good to be gained by taking responsibility. If you haven't been finishing your tasks, create a program to ensure you get them done in good time. You will feel good about it and reduce the weight of such a thought.

- ***If unreasonable, figure out the distortion:*** On the other hand, if the thought is unreasonable, pin it down to the type of distortion it is so you can use the means discussed above to burst it. Usually, people have a tendency to have a certain pattern. You could be having fairness fallacies or mental filtering, among others. Identify what pattern you are displaying, then work on overcoming the distortion.

- ***Develop a reasonable thought:*** Having identified that you have cognitive distortions and that your thoughts are unreasonable, it is time to come up with a more reasonable thought to take the place of the distorted one. For example, instead of saying you are stupid, you can acknowledge that you are semi-skilled in data analysis and could use more training in the field. Remember to write it down to give it life and permanence. If you cannot think of anything, think about what a friend would say.

- ***Recheck that distress temperature:*** Check your level of distress again to see if it had dropped by a few levels. Appreciate even the slightest drop as it signifies that you are moving in the right direction.

- ***Practice:*** Similar to cognitive restructuring, gaining a hold of your thoughts is not an easy exercise. You will be required to keep practicing and teaching yourself to think positive thoughts until it becomes natural for you. There is hope. You can do it. Over time and with commitment, you can burst those cognitive distortions that threaten your peace and happiness.

Chapter Summary

In this chapter, we have learned about cognitive distortions, bursting them and how to slow down their intrusion.

- Cognitive distortions refer to repeated ways of thinking that often are negative and inaccurate.
- Some of the most common cognitive distortions include mental filtering, overgeneralization, polarized thinking, catastrophizing, personalization, emotional reasoning, labeling and 'should' statements.
- You can break away from cognitive distortions by using methods, such as cost-benefit analysis, definition, experiments, use of semantics and re-attribution, among others.
- The key to breaking from cognitive distortions is identifying the issue, and then going on to find its rationality. In many cases, you will realize that the thoughts are incorrect and irrational.
- Always replace the irrational thought with a more accurate and rational thought.

In the next chapter, you will learn about journaling and the benefits that come with putting things down in writing, as well as how it helps to improve your mental health.

CHAPTER FIVE

Technique 3 – Write it Down

By now, you have realized that we are constantly talking about the need to write down the thoughts. You may be thinking that these thoughts occur all the time, and you have no time to keep writing them down. As inconveniencing as it sounds, it is good practice to note down those thoughts as they occur. Doing so later will mean that you will struggle to understand your mood at that time and remember the particular thoughts and meaning. When you catch them raw, you are in a better place to articulate them and put down the feelings as they occur.

Think back to when you were younger, a pre-teen, teen or even a young adult. Chances are high that you kept a diary hidden under your bed. In it were your innermost thoughts, challenges and experiences. You wrote down the thoughts that mattered and those that you could not share with another person. You knew you could trust the diary to be part of your thoughts without any judgement. You were free to write down any thoughts. and the diary absorbed them, making you feel lighter yet protected.

As you grew older, you probably stopped keeping a diary and thoughts began crashing into you. The weight that the diary took has not found another home and so is held within you. While you may have friends and family that you can talk to, sometimes you may have deep thoughts that you would rather not share. Writing down your experiences, thoughts and moods makes them not only clearer but also helps you gain control of them and benefits your mental health.

What does writing it down mean?

Also known as journaling, it is a practice of writing down thoughts and events to meet your set goals and improve the quality of life. Each person has a unique way of writing things down and a particular reason, but the outcome has been mostly positive. You may have heard someone ask you about your dreams and goals, and then inquire if you had them written down. By writing them down, you can reach your goals because you are clear on what you want to achieve and can craft a way of how to do just that. Journaling helps in clearing your mind, connecting thoughts, feelings, and behaviors, as well as buffering or reducing effects of mental disorders.

How does it work?

Writing your thoughts and feelings down uses the rational and analytical left side of the brain, giving space and room for the touchy-feely and creative right side to be free to play and wander. The effect is that your creativity flourishes, expanding the cathartic and making a positive impact on your well-being.

Benefits of Journaling for Mental Health

There are many benefits you get from developing a habit of expressive writing. Some of them include:

- Managing anxiety
- Coping with depression
- Stress reduction
- Helping in the prioritization of fears, concerns and problems
- Daily tracking of symptoms to recognize triggers and learn coping and control strategies
- Identification of negative behaviors and thoughts
- Provision of opportunities for positive self-talk
- Improving your working memory
- Reducing intrusive thoughts and avoidance symptoms
- Boosting your mood
- Enhancing a sense of well-being

- Clearing and calming the mind
- Opening your mind to your successes and struggles
- Tracking your mental-health progress
- Acts as a release for pent-up feelings
- Helps to enhance self-awareness
- Helps in considering multiple options and planning

Writing down our thoughts enhances your mental health by guiding you to confront emotions that were previously inhibited, thus reducing the stress that comes with the inhibitions. Further, it helps you to process difficult events. For example, if you are grieving the loss of a loved one, writing it down helps you open up about how terrible it feels and to process the event. You also have the opportunity to develop a coherent narrative about the event and your experiences and, hence, you can deal with its trauma. Having this time to intimately deal with your emotions is crucial to healing.

In case you are facing a traumatic experience, writing it down enhances your mental health by making you more self-aware. You can also easily detect unhealthy thinking and behavioral patterns that may be sneaking in, which, in turn, allows you to have more control so you can put things in order before it is late.

An additional benefit of journaling is that it helps you embrace a positive mindset and move from a negative one, since you are aware of what is going on within you. In essence, it strengthens your cognitive functioning.

Tips for Constructive Journaling

For you to harness the benefits that come with journaling, it has to be done effectively. While you may choose to dump words on a page, you may feel better, but you will certainly miss out on all the other amazing benefits, such as reduced stress, intrusive thoughts, anxiety and depression. Here are some tips you can follow when writing down your thoughts for mental health:

a) *Have some private space:* You are about to note down some of your most private and intimate thoughts, and you certainly do not need people craning their necks to read them. Find a personalized space that does not have distractions.
b) *Make it a habit:* When starting out, you can write down your thoughts three to four times a week but work on increasing that to every day.

If possible, write down when an intrusive thought occurs. There are now smartphone applications that you can use for this purpose, so you don't need a pen and paper.

c) *Take time to reflect:* After writing, take time to go through what you wrote quietly and objectively so you can balance yourself. Sometimes you do not even have to think about what you wrote but try to relax and balance your thoughts, particularly, when the thoughts are quite heavy.

d) *No need to be specific:* As much as it would be best to capture each thought and place it within an event, you do not have to do that. If you are working to overcome trauma, you do not have to write the specific event that caused the trauma. All you have to do is write about what you feel at that moment and what feels right to be written.

e) *Structure as you please:* The focal point of journaling is to get your thoughts and moods out of you and onto a page. There is no set structure or formula on how to do that. Write it however you feel is best.

f) *Ensure it's private:* Make sure to keep your journal private and away from unwanted eyes and hands. Knowing that it is safe makes you feel safe, too, and encourages you to keep writing. If you have to share or discuss it, then you can do so with your therapist.

WRITE Guidelines

A set of guidelines that has been useful for me in this journey are the WRITE guidelines, as they are simple to remember and effective in journaling. All you have to keep in mind is WRITE.

- ***W stands for What to write about.*** There are no restrictions on What to write, but some people find it difficult to write anything down and end up staring at a blank page for hours. Write about your current feelings, thoughts and anything and everything that is going on in your life. You can even write about your goals and what you are striving to achieve.
- ***R stands for Review.*** Writing is not enough to get you to understand your inner thoughts. Take some time to Review as well as Reflect on what you are writing. You need to be calm, still, collected and focused for this step. If you are feeling unsettled, you can opt for a little meditation or mindfulness. It is best to use 'I' statements, such as "I feel…" or "I think…". Try also to keep your writing in the present, for example,

"Today I have been in a foul mood." "Now I feel…"

- ***I stands for Investigate.*** You need to investigate your feelings and thoughts as you write. Sometimes the mind may start wandering around instead of staying focused, especially if you are running out of things to write. In such instances, take time to go through what you have written and add any thoughts or events you may have left out. Alternatively, you can take time for re-focusing through meditation or mindfulness. Once you feel ready, keep writing.

- ***T stands for Time.*** Have a goal for how much time you want to spend writing on the minimum. Initially, even a minute may seem a lot, but set a goal and work toward it. For example, you can choose to spend at least five minutes each day writing. Note down the time as you begin to write alongside the projected end time. You can set an alarm to keep you aware of the time. Over time, as you get used to writing, you will begin to enjoy how therapeutic it is, and you will look forward to the activity.

- ***E stands for Exit.*** After writing, do not dump your journal and bail out until the next time. No, you need to exit strategically and with a level of soul-searching. Go through what you have written and reflect on it. Sum up what you have read as a conclusion to your thoughts and an observation. For example, you can note that, "As I read this, I note that I have been focusing only on the negative side of life." You can also take this opportunity to come up with action points for you to commit to. For example, "I will be intentional in drawing out the positive things that happen." Also write your action items down so you can follow through.

Be You, Do You

Many people take up journaling for different reasons. Some write for fun, others for work, while many people find that it provides an avenue to express themselves. When you are writing for your mental health, it is important that you focus on the objective of getting better, but do not allow it to be a source of unnecessary pressure.

As with everything else, the beginning is bound to be challenging. You may find that you do not know what to write. Now is not the time to worry about it but to get you started. Write about anything; how you feel, what your thoughts are and even events that happened.

As you mature into it, you will learn to focus your writing on relevant thoughts and reflect on them. You will even go further to analyze and realize where you went wrong and work on correcting that. The idea is to start writing.

Do not aim for perfection; aim for self-expression. Ensure that you are honest with yourself and are able to look deep within you and articulate your feelings and thoughts. Over time, refine the process as per the guidelines, and you will witness the power of writing.

I remember my first days of writing were particularly hard because I had never kept a diary, even as a teenager. However, I have learned to enjoy writing down my thoughts and feelings. I consider it as having a second non-judgmental me to go through my day with me, combing through my deepest thoughts and reflecting on the struggles and successes. When I am overcome with thoughts that I cannot share with others, I am happy to know that I have somewhere I can pour them and not have to worry about consequences. I come out feeling lighter and happier.

Chapter Summary

In this chapter, we have looked at journaling, the associated benefits of writing down your thoughts and feelings and the best way to do it. In summary:

- Effective journaling involves writing down your thoughts and feelings, as well as experiences, and taking time to reflect on them.
- Journaling has numerous benefits, including providing an avenue to release pent-up emotions, managing anxiety, prioritization of fears and concerns, and opportunities for positive self-talk that breaks negative thoughts.
- You can apply the WRITE guideline in journaling that calls for knowing What to write, Reflecting, Investigating, Time and Exiting strategically.
- At the end of the day, write as you want first before building in the reflecting and going forward.
- Start today and keep growing. Practice makes perfect.

In the next chapter, you will learn about another useful CBT technique: exposure and response prevention.

CHAPTER SIX

Technique 4 – Exposure and Response Prevention

You may not welcome the idea of exposing yourself to the same things that trigger anxiety and obsessions or send you into a full panic attack. Don't run off yet, hear me out. Exposing yourself to the triggers and them being beneficial is what exposure and response prevention is all about. My initial encounter with this CBT technique had me all packed up and wearing my running shoes. There was no way I was going to put myself through that. You probably have the same thought, but take some time and let's explore how this can help you heal and find peace.

In Exposure and Response Prevention (ERP), the Exposure aspect means that you expose yourself to objects, images, situations and thoughts that ruffle your feathers, making you nervous, anxious and bringing up all your obsessions. The second part of ERP, the Response Prevention, calls for you to not give in to all that ruffling and try to remain calm even after all the triggers are on. I know all this sounds scary, bearing in mind how our triggers bring out the worst in us.

You can think of those triggers as alarm bells. Once an alarm goes off, it calls for your attention and tells you it is time to spring into action. For instance, if, when you are sleeping and your security alarm system goes off, you know there is an intruder and to call the police even if it's the cat that set it off. No matter what sets off the alarm, we respond in a similar way, seeking to protect us and our families.

Similarly, these triggers are supposed to get your attention, more like a warning and for you to get ready to deal with whatever is coming. However, with mental illnesses, the triggers sound like danger to us and make us react in a compulsive way. You do not even get time to investigate if it is a real break-in or a bat that landed on the window triggering the alarm system. Often, we allow any trigger, even the minute ones, to sound like seven gunmen broke down the door with guns blaring. Most of the time, those triggers you allow to hold you captive are negligible, yet you make them sound like a catastrophic and terrifying threat. You may find that, when the alarm goes off, it communicates danger instead of asking you to pay attention to the fact that there could be potential danger.

Understandably, it may be difficult to make a decision on starting the ERP technique, as it feels like you are deliberately exposing yourself to danger. However, through ERP, you will be able to change your brain functioning. Have you realized that most of the time that you feel like you are in danger you actually know that you are not? In those moments, you are unable to control your reactions and end up thinking the worst and behaving similarly. Starting on the ERP journey will help you take control of your thoughts and emotions and consequently your behavior. The beginning is bound to be challenging, so it is best to start off with a qualified therapist. After a while, you will find it easy to undertake ERP by yourself.

Is it Effective?

Before you put yourself through what appears to be torture, although I assure you it isn't, you may be interested to know if it is worth it. Yes, it is worth the effort. There are many studies that have found ERP to be effective, particularly in the long-term treatment of OCD and anxiety. Unlike medication, where the symptoms tend to return after the dosage wears off, the effects of the success of ERP lasts beyond the treatment. Besides, the Emotional Processing Theory asserts that there are powerful lessons involved in the ERP treatment method.

How does it work?

The mechanism by which ERP works is best explained by two cognitive models: the inhibitory-learning model and habituation-learning model.

People mainly develop disorders from misinterpreting the significance of normally occurring intrusive thoughts that we all experience at different points in life. Furthermore, having dysfunctional thoughts, such as overestimation of threat, search for perfectionism, a need to control thoughts and an inflated sense of responsibility for the protection of self and others, all fuel OCD by making you interpret intrusive thoughts as significant and dangerous.

ERP helps to disconfirm those distorted beliefs by exposing you to the stimuli. If you have an intense fear of crossing roads as you expect to be knocked down, then repeatedly having to cross a road and subsequently *not* getting knocked down will alleviate that fear. Additionally, ERP also breaks the conditioned response that you have between obsessions and compulsions.

Habituation-Learning Model

Habituation is the reduction of fearful emotions and anxious psychological responses to frequent stimuli. The habituation-learning model works by causing a shift in the patient's belief system, such as overestimation of the risk associated, and by causing a reduction in the link between the threat appraisal and the belief.

Naturally, we tend to respond to stimuli through the fight-or-flight response. However, during ERP, you realize that the sympathetic nervous system that is responsible for anxiety's physiological part cannot indefinitely maintain the fight-or-flight response. In habituation, after some exposure time, approximately an hour after exposure, the parasympathetic nervous system gets triggered to help in settling down its sympathetic counterpart. The process happens regardless of how you cognitively interpret the situation. You therefore have to correct the cognitive schemas, even in the face of a feared stimulus in order to achieve homeostasis.

Habituation means that you have to change your behavior first so that the cognitions are modified then the emotions also change. In simple language, habituation calls for you to feed corrective information into your mind so that the body can settle down, your behavior can normalize and then your emotions become stable.

For example, if you are afraid of dirt and germs and associate them with the ability to contract a deadly incurable illness, then you will find that you avoid touching certain things, such as the trash can, public washroom handles, sinks and other highly contaminated areas. During the event, you don't keep washing your hands over and over again. In habituation, the therapist will expose you to those surfaces that you dread touching and make you touch them. You may be asked to touch the sink, the trash can and the washroom door handle; that is Exposure. Even as you feel like your world is exploding with germs, the therapist might then ask you to join her for a meal without allowing you to wash your hands even once, let alone seven times. Having a meal with unscrubbed hands may prove to be the real test, as you can imagine all the germs crawling on you. Here, that is the Response Prevention.

Initially, you will realize, as you touch those seemingly dirty surfaces, that your anxiety levels are likely to spike, but will begin to stabilize the more you touch the surfaces. After eating a meal and not immediately falling sick, you will also realize that the fear is exaggerated. You will then modify your earlier thinking and lessen the likelihood of contracting deadly diseases from dirty surfaces. You will become more accommodating of dirt than before, as you have seen that nothing much happened. Repeated exposure to the stimuli may even dissipate the fear.

Inhibitory-Learning Model

The inhibitory-learning model of ERP, unlike habituation, proposes that the association between the obsession/stimuli and the fear continues to exist and the links do not break. Instead, exposure to the stimuli brings in safety-based and new inhibitory associations. The model aims to ensure that patients learn that, at times, their feared outcomes occur when exposed to the stimulus, but other times the outcome they so fear does not occur. Thus, they have to develop both cognitive and emotional flexibility to prepare and deal with whatever outcome.

In essence, you learn to be more tolerant toward distress as well as being in contact with what is presently happening, rather than sitting back and waiting for the homeostasis process to kick in, as in habituation. Here, you do not sit back and wait for nature to take its course but rather are prepared for the possibility of your fears coming alive or not. You react to the immediate situation and what is happening, rather than freeze and wait for the body to try and stabilize. You invest in the present rather than in a would-be outcome.

The inhibitory-learning model helps you build adaptiveness by shifting focus from possible future-oriented outcomes to the present experiences and values.

Besides, it gives you power and control by putting you in charge. You learn that the choice to decide on where to place your focus is in your hands. You can focus on what is happening presently or the future possibilities without necessarily having to wait for habituation to occur. You make the decision on where to place your thoughts and energy, which is empowering.

Conducting ERP

You may want to conduct your initial ERP with a therapist. However, there is no limit to the number of places that it can be done. Depending on the intensity level of the illness, ERP can be in an outpatient or residential treatment setting, partial hospitalization or even at home. Whatever your intensity level, there are some elements that form part of the ERP process.

- **Assessment and Planning for Treatment:** The clinician or a relevant health-care provider carries out assessment and provides you with psychoeducation. You learn about the available treatment methods and discuss your symptoms.
- **Trigger identification:** You work alongside your therapist to identify external objects, people and situations that trigger anxiety and obsessive thoughts. You also look internally into your physiological reactions and thoughts to see

which ones cause distress and obsessive behavior.

- **Specify the content of obsessions and compulsions:** At this point, you also discuss how the two functionally relate, as well as identify the feared outcome, such as dying or contracting an illness. If you like to wash your hands 10 times, you may have a fear of getting infected if you do not, or you simply feel disgusted by dirt on your hands and will keep washing until when you feel clean.
- **Rank situations:** Together, rank the situations from the least distressing to the most distressing, based on your level of fear.
- **Coaching:** Having established a good background, it is time for you to undergo coaching by being exposed to situations or objects on your fear hierarchy while you work at not engaging in compulsions. You may also be exposed to imaginary situations where you envision your feared outcomes.
- **Learning to cope:** As you go through the exposure, you begin to realize that, in most cases, the worst scenario (in your head) does not occur. You do not fall ill after touching the dirty surface nor does that imaginary situation lead to the perceived consequences.

- **Post-exposure processing:** After each session, you will review the experiences, the violation of the expectations and the lessons learned.
- **Homework:** In most cases, the therapist will ask you to continually practice exposures on your own as you learned to eliminate daily rituals. You will realize that over time you begin to move up your fear hierarchy and are able to literally face most of them and easily confront distressing situations.

I do understand that literally facing your fears may not be something that you are willing to try. However, it is a great way to address them head on. Besides, I will tell you that it sounds harder than it actually is. Touching the first dirty surface is harder than touching the fifth one because, by then, your distress will be lower. Having not to respond is what I found more challenging, but you learn and realize that you can actually go through life without the unnecessary compulsions. The more you are exposed to the stimuli, the lesser the distress level until you get to the point where it falls on the lower side of your fear hierarchy.

As earlier mentioned, you may want to start ERP with a therapist for encouragement before venturing out on your own. Things get easier with each exposure, and the burden is lifted. You will enjoy life without the obsessions and compulsions.

Chapter Summary

In this chapter, we have learned about the ERP method of mastering your brain and overcoming anxiety and OCD. In particular, we have learned that:

- ERP stands for Exposure and Response Prevention.
- By being exposed to the stimuli that trigger anxiety and OCD, you learn to prevent response and therefore gain control.
- You can use either the habituation- or inhibitory-learning models.
- Habituation calls for your mind to be exposed to the trigger until it automatically begins homeostasis while in the inhibitory-learning model, you learn that you have choices. You can either take what is presently happening or expect the worst possible outcome.
- It is advisable that you start ERP with a therapist before attempting it on your own. Initially, it can be intimidating for many people to face their triggers.

In the next chapter, you will learn another CBT technique that calls for you to relax. While it sounds like a simple task for ordinary people, it can be pretty difficult for anyone battling any mental illness. There is the yearning to be able to relax. Let us learn how to do so.

CHAPTER SEVEN

Technique 5 – Relax

You are probably thinking that it is easier said than done. When battling mental illnesses, particularly anxiety, depression and intrusive thoughts, you may find it difficult to relax. There are 10s of things wrong and 1,000 more that could potentially go wrong. You are likely always in a state of turmoil, fighting one thing or another, and it is tiring. The good news is that you can relax! Yes, even you are entitled to relaxation; it is not for the chosen few.

When faced with stressful situations, we tend to respond using the stress response, which comes naturally to help us survive like in prehistoric times when our ancestors had to employ the stress response to live through floods or even animal attacks. Despite the change in lifestyle over the years, we still face threatening situations that set off our stress responses. I am certain you can name several occasions when you feel the familiar pounding of the heart, increased breathing and the tension fill the muscles. At such times, relaxation is the last thing on your mind.

Since it is not possible to do away with all the stressors in life, it is important to learn how to activate the relaxation response. The relaxation response technique was first developed at Harvard Medical School in the 1970s by Dr. Herbert Benson, who was a cardiologist. The stress response is the opposite of the relaxation response. The relaxation response denotes profound rest. It may sound like a dream now, but with regular practice you can make a relaxed well of calm that you can tap into whenever necessary.

Relaxation Techniques

There are various relaxation techniques in CBT that you can learn. The key is to find what works well for you. Let us explore some of the techniques you can add to your daily routine to help you relax.

Breathing Techniques

Did you know that there are several ways that you can breathe to reduce anxiety and stress, improve your lungs and help you to relax? To add breathing exercises to your daily life, you must make time for it. As little as two to five minutes a day are enough to make a difference. You can practice several times a day to get the best out of these breathing exercises. Some of the exercises include:

- ***Pursed lip breathing:*** Here, the aim is to slow down your breathing by ensuring that you apply deliberate effort. All you have to do is relax both the neck and shoulders, then with the mouth closed, gently inhale through the nose for two counts. Purse or pucker the lips as if whistling, then slowly exhale by blowing the air through the puckered lips for four counts.

- ***Diaphragmatic breathing:*** If you need to need to seriously relax and feel rested, all you have to do is practice diaphragmatic breathing for about five to 10 minutes a day. You need to lie down on your back with your head on a pillow and knees bent slightly. Take one hand and place it below your ribcage while the other goes on your upper chest so you can feel the diaphragm move. Gently inhale through the nose, so you feel the stomach press into the hand while keeping the other hand as still as possible. Exhale through pursed lips keeping your upper hand still and tightening your stomach muscle. To make it more difficult, you can put a book on your abdomen. Once you learn to belly breathe lying down, you can do it while seated on a chair and eventually do it whenever and wherever you want.

- ***Breath-focus technique:*** In this technique, there are focus words and phrases in use. The idea is to choose a focus word that makes you feel relaxed, smile or feel neutral, and focus on it repeatedly. Examples include such words as relax, peace and joy. Practice your breath focus for about 10 minutes a session, then work your way up. For this exercise, you can either sit or lie down in a place that is comfortable, then, without trying to change how you are breathing, bring awareness to your breath. Next, alternate between deep breaths and normal ones, paying attention to how your abdomen expands as you deeply inhale and practice deep breathing. Place a hand below your belly button, relax and notice the rise and fall with each inhalation and exhalation, respectively. Loudly sigh with each exhalation. Start breath-focusing by combining deep breathing with a focus word, phrase or imagery that will help you to relax. For example, you can assume that the air you inhale is calmness and peace, while the one you exhale is anxiety and tension.

- ***Alternate nostril breathing:*** Popularly known as nodi shodhana, it is best practiced before meals and is effective for enhancing cardiovascular function and lowering heart rate. If you are congested or sick, you may want to avoid this exercise, since you need to keep your breath smooth and even throughout. The exercise is simple. Find a comfortable position when seated and lift your right hand to the nose only pressing the first and middle fingers to the palm while the rest are extended. Gently close the right nostril after an exhale, inhaling through the left nostril before closing it with the right ring and pinky fingers. In essence, the thumb closes the right nostril while the ring and pinky fingers close the left nostril. Next, release the thumb and exhale through the right nostril before inhaling again through it, then closing it. Open the left nostril and exhale. Keep the cycle going for up to five minutes. Remember to end the session with an exhalation on the left side.

- *Lion's breath:* No, you are not turning into a lion, but wouldn't you want to have its energy? The lion's breath not only energizes you but also relieves tension in your face and chest. Simply find a comfortable seated position either on your heels or cross-legged. Spread your fingers wide and press the palms against your knees then inhale deeply through the nose with eyes wide open. Open your mouth wide, stick out your tongue and bring its tip towards the chin. Next, contract your frontal throat muscles and exhale through the mouth producing a long "ha" sound. Then, turn your gaze to the space at your nose's tip or between your eyebrows. Repeat this two to three times and feel the energy flow within you.

- *Equal breathing:* If you are feeling particularly unbalanced, then this is the breathing exercise for you. The focus is on making your inhales and exhales the same length, steady and smooth to give you balance and equanimity. The breath length should also be neither too difficult nor easy, but also fast enough to maintain through the practice, usually for 3-5 counts. For this, find a comfortable seated position, then use your nose to breathe in and out. Count the time during each inhale, and ensure the exhale gets similar time. You can choose to have a slight pause after each inhale and exhale. Keep up the cycle for at least five minutes.

- *Coherent/resonant breathing:* Here, you take five full breaths each minute by inhaling and exhaling for a count of five. Resonant breathing not only maximizes your HRV (Heart Rate Variability), but it also reduces stress, as well as symptoms of depression. All you have to do is inhale for a count to five and exhale for a similar count, then keep going for a few minutes.

- ***Deep breathing:*** You may have heard the phrase, "Take a deep breath." Taking a deep breath helps to keep you centered and relaxed, and it sure works. You can do this while sitting or standing. Drawing your elbows back slightly allows your chest to expand. Inhale deeply through the nose and hold for a count of 55 before slowly releasing the breath through the nose. You can repeat this until you feel sufficiently relaxed and able to deal with whatever the situation.

- ***Sitali breath:*** This is also a good breathing exercise for relaxing your mind. Find a comfortable seated position, then stick your tongue out and curl it bringing in the outer edges together. If your tongue is stubborn and refuses to oblige, simply purse your lips. Inhale through the mouth, and exhale through the nose. Repeat the cycle for about five minutes.

- ***Humming bee breath:*** If you ever need instant calm, then this is the breathing exercise for you.

It also helps to relieve anxiety, anger and frustration. The only flip side is that you do need to sound like a humming bee, so choose your place well for this exercise. After picking a comfortable seated position, relax your face and close your eyes, then put the first finger on the tragus cartilage, which partially covers the ear canal. Breathe in and, as you breathe out, gently press into the cartilage, then hum loudly. Keep going until you feel comfortable or calm enough.

Mindfulness Meditation

For those suffering from anxiety, pain and depression, you can get reprieve and be able to relax through mindfulness meditation. You only need to find a comfortable sitting position, then focus on your breathing. The key thing here is to bring your mind's attention to the present moment. It helps if you find a good relaxing place like a park, forest or the riverbank to do this. Focus on the current moment without allowing your mind to drift to the past and what you could have done or should have done. Also, this is not the time to start worrying about the future, its concerns and what it will bring. The time now is to focus on the present, taking in the environment and allowing yourself to relax.

Many people have experienced the joy of mindful meditation, making it one of the most popular methods of relaxation. I am also a great supporter of this technique as it is one of the surest ways to breathe in, take in the moment and relax.

Tai Chi, Yoga and Qigong

Not only do these three ancient arts come loaded with physical and beauty benefits, but they also have the ability to focus your thoughts in a way that distracts racing thoughts and helps you to relax. Besides, they also enhance your balance and flexibility. If you generally do not lead an active life or have health problems, you may want to stay away from these. However, with a good trainer, you can begin from the beginner level and build up as you experience both mind relaxation and fitness. It is recommended that you check with your doctor before beginning these exercises.

Guided scenery

We all naturally want to associate with good things, soothing scenes and experiences. However, life throws many other difficult experiences and situations at us that can potentially push us into a world of negativity and self-doubt. At such times, you can pull out the gilded scenery technique. Here you conjure up images of soothing places, scenes and experiences that can help you to focus and relax. The good news is that there are different applications and recordings available online that have calming scenes for you to choose from. Ensure you choose what calms you down, has personal significance and makes you feel positive. Through guided imagery, you reinforce positivity within yourself, keeping away the negative thoughts and helping you to relax. You focus your attention on the image, or scene and relax into the moment clearing your mind of the negativity and going into a positive and soothing mood. The technique is particularly useful and calming to those with intrusive thoughts or who find it difficult to conjure up positive mental images.

Repetitive Prayer

If you are one of those people who are not very keen on religion, this may not be the best technique for you. However, you can attest that in times of need, darkness and hopelessness, we all tend to say a prayer. The idea behind this technique is to silently repeat a phrase or a short prayer while performing breath focus. If you are particularly religious or spiritual, you will draw more meaning from this technique as it appeals to your spirit, as well as the mind. You can even opt to add some of the religious items, like a rosary or praying beads, to make the experience wholesome. Adding breathing exercises ensures that the combination is relaxing. If you are not quite the spiritual or the religious type, you can repeat a positive phrase or a paragraph over and over until you feel relaxed and at peace. The constant repeating helps your mind to focus and absorb the positive message and leave aside the intrusive thoughts or anxiety.

Body Scan

There are no big machines to get into for the scan. Instead, this technique combines breath focus with focused muscle relaxation. You need to start with deep breathing, as we learned earlier on, until you feel sufficiently comfortable. The next step is to focus on either a group of muscles or one part of the body at any given time. You mentally release any tension that you may feel in these muscles or part of the body while still on breath focus. The reason it is called a body scan is because you move from one part to the next, releasing the tension until you feel relaxed everywhere. In the process, you will grow aware of the connection between body and mind and appreciate how interrelated they are. Pay special attention to the areas that you feel are strained, like your eyes or head. As soon as you are done, you will be amazed at how light you feel and how much mental weight you will have shed, leaving you relaxed.

Exercise

Most people who work out regularly know the benefits of exercise. However, if you are not one of them, you may consider it to be more trouble. Exercise is one of the most effective ways of combating stress, anxiety, depression and intrusive thoughts, while gaining the benefits of having a healthier, fit and more beautiful body. As weird as it sounds, putting yourself through physical stress relieves mental stress and helps you to relax and feel good.

By exercising you lower your body's stress hormones, like cortisol, while promoting the release of endorphins, which make you feel good, are natural painkillers and improve your mood. Additionally, exercise improves your sleep quality, something that those battling with mental illness would really appreciate. Sleep can be elusive, and even when present, it involves much tossing and turning. Exercise can sort the sleep issue making you relaxed and energetic when you get up. Moreover, exercise comes with a body to die for, one that you are proud of and thus boosts your confidence, contributing to your mental well-being.

With exercise, you do not have to become a top athlete, although that is also welcome. You need to choose an exercise routine that works for you, something that you enjoy, and you can do often. For example, you can begin taking walks that help to soothe you and appreciate the environment. You can also opt for swimming, yoga, hiking or even dancing. Find whatever exercise makes you happy. You do not have to know how to do it; enjoy the learning process and notice how relaxed you get, losing both physical and mental baggage.

Light A Candle

You do not have to be a hopeless romantic to light a candle. Get a candle with a soothing scent, like lavender, rose, sandalwood, neroli, vetiver, Roman chamomile, Geranium, Ylang ylang, Bergamot, Orange or Frankincense. The art of using these scents in improving your mood is referred to as aromatherapy, which has been known to improve sleep, reduce anxiety and make you relaxed. The calming scents will help you relax and lift off any negative emotions. You can light a candle while taking a shower, or even during a delicious meal or in your living room or bedroom.

Write It Down

We have already talked in depth about the topic of journaling. Writing down your thoughts and emotions is one of the most effective ways of relaxing, as it lifts the mental stress and gives you an opportunity to replace the negative thoughts with positive ones.

Join Great Company

Often people get stressed, anxious, sink further into depression and host all their intrusive thoughts because of being alone and brooding. You can easily escape all these and enjoy fun times with family and friends. You have to carefully choose those that come with a good vibe and bring out the best in you. Having good social support is a great way to pull through mental illness and stressful situations. Women particularly benefit from social support, as they release oxytocin, which is a natural stress reliever.

Alternatively, you can choose to spend time with a support group for people battling mental illness. Ensure that you are with people that understand your condition and urge you to get out of it or those who have done so successfully. The idea is to keep your outlook positive.

Say No

Sit and think back to the hardest times you have had, and you will realize that they most likely emanated from your inability to say no. You may find that you pile your plate too high with other people's problems, concerns and activities that you can say no to. You could be financially constrained because you gave your money to someone else. Your work life may be stressful because you are intent on helping others.

Only take on what is comfortable for you to do, and say no to everything that will put unnecessary stress on you. You will find that your life is more relaxed, and you are more productive and less stressed.

Laugh

When you are laughing, your worries, anxieties, stresses and stressors disappear. There is relaxing power in laughing, in addition to relieving stress and tension. Laughing also puts you in a good mood, enabling you to relax.

Call that one friend who cracks you up or hang out with some good friends and family. If you are not in the mood for dealing with people, watch a funny show on TV or even those hilarious clips on YouTube. You should be happy and relaxed in no time.

Chapter Summary

In this chapter, we have looked at various ways you can relax even when you feel like the weight of the world is on your shoulder. We learned that:

- Breathing exercises are some of the most effective ways of relaxing. There are many different modes of breathing for relaxation, including the lion's breath and deep breathing.
- You can also engage in mindful meditation, yoga or even guided scenery, among others.
- You do not have to use one of these techniques. You can try different combinations until you find what works best for you.

In the next chapter, you will learn another CBT technique that can help you in fighting anxiety, depression and intrusive thoughts. It is simply by having fun!

CHAPTER EIGHT

Technique 6 – Have Fun

Have you ever realized how our activities influence our mood? For instance, if you listen to sad songs, you get sad and fall into a low mood. On the other hand, if you listen to lively music, you will end up dancing to it and generally feeling happy, alive and energetic. If you spend most of your time among negative people or depressing situations, you are likely to end up feeling stressed or depressed. Looking at the trend, therefore, it is important to fill your days with positivity and to schedule activities that you enjoy. In a world filled with stress, you have to create a small piece of heaven for yourself. One way of learning to do so is through a CBT technique called activity scheduling and behavioral activation.

What is Activity Scheduling and Behavioral Activation?

Most of the activities that we have to do for our survival are mainly challenging and not very pleasant. You may need to find a way to create some positivity and fun in your life by scheduling as well as participating in positive events that boost your mood. Activity scheduling and behavioral activation is an evidence-based CBT technique that is effective in the reduction of a number of mental-health symptoms.

When you are suffering from a mental-health condition, you may want to stay away from people, preferring to wallow in your pain and not deal with any social issues. You will tend to isolate yourself and cancel engaging activities, even those that you previously enjoyed, as well as decline invitations by colleagues, friends and family. While you may think of this as a way of reducing pressure on yourself, it increases your depression making it intense and last longer and subsequently making you want to isolate yourself even more.

A good way of breaking the cycle is identifying an activity that boosts your mood, like swimming, having dinner with a friend, watching a live match or even going to the gym. Your therapist can work with you in picking a positive and engaging activity to do. The therapist, however, does not help in picking any random and fun activity. He helps in the identification of the value of these activities and rank them. For instance, he may check how work, volunteering, family, friendship, intimacy, entertainment or health, among others, are of value to you. He will then help you to gather activities that support what you value the most. For example, if you value friendships, you may be interested in having coffee with a friend. On the other hand, if you value health and fitness, going to the gym may be most appealing to you.

Once you engage in the activity, you can review how it affected your mood. If you find that you are feeling much better than before, then you can continue scheduling the activity or find a similar one to keep your mood light.

How does it work?

Scheduling an activity that is pleasant and fun can help you be better by providing you with something to look forward to. The boost in mood starts immediately from the planning stage and all the way to the time for the activity.

Engaging in a pleasant activity that adds value to your life will certainly cause you to experience a bright mood. You will feel great at having done something beneficial yet fun which can help you break out of the terrible mood you have sustained for so long. You may find that you are now willing to engage in other similar activities.

How to effectively enhance Activity Scheduling and Behavioral Activation

Activity scheduling and behavioral activation may sound like a simple coping skill, but you may find yourself struggling to get it done particularly when unmotivated. After some time in isolation, you get used to your own presence, and breaking away from this cycle can be pretty difficult. Below are some of the ways that can get you started on scheduling pleasant activities.

- ***Go for activities that are personally important:*** Sometimes, we are tempted to live for other people. You may choose to have a coffee date with a friend because that friend has been pushing for it or choose an activity that will make your partner happy. Remember, the focal person here is you so choose activities that are of importance to you to get your motivation up. Ensure that you go for activities that you are connected to and engaged with and that bring you joy. The objective is for you to have fun, feel good and fulfill some of your desires.

- ***Choose specific activities with measurable progress:*** Do not opt for blanket activities but rather choose something with which you can easily track the progress. You have to be able to know that you completed a task and review it. For example, instead of planning to get fit, be specific. Plan to either go to the gym for an hour or jump rope for 10 minutes. You can hold yourself accountable and be proud of what you achieve, which will further motivate you to go further. Achieving your goals will also lift your mood.

- ***Start from the easiest to the most difficult activities:*** When you are anxious about something or generally feeling low, you may find behavioral activation as being quite hard. A way to ease you into it is to just get started. If you are to go out for coffee, you can begin by simply taking a shower, then pat yourself on the back for that. If you don't get moving, you can easily find that avoidance behaviors begin to set in. List all your activities from the easiest and begin with that. As you keep going, you will realize it is not as hard as you thought it would be. Soon, you will get immersed in the activity and go on to complete it. Additionally, starting with the easy tasks ensures that you do not get overwhelmed.

- ***Ask for support:*** Occasionally, it is hard to pull yourself out of the rut that comes with mental illness. You may want to attend to those fun activities, but you lack the strength and will to do so. At such times, do not be afraid to ask for help from people in your support circle. Tell a trusted friend or family member what you plan to achieve during the week and ask them to be your accountability partner. They can check in on how far you have gone, encourage you and be your cheerleader. In the end, you get to have fun, even if there are small steps at the start.

- *Spice it up!:* They say that variety is the spice of life, so don't be boring. The whole objective is to get you out of that gloomy room and get some adrenaline and feel-good hormones flowing through you. Mix up different types of activities across varying life sectors, like fitness, entertainment and work. The more activities you plan, the more likely you are to have more fun and get into a better mood. Besides, doing one thing repetitively will wear you down and slump you back to the world of gloom.

- *Be mindful:* Have you driven home, yet your mind is elsewhere and full of other things? Similarly, you can be engaging in a fun activity, yet you are not having any fun. Your mind is engaged elsewhere worrying about your future or ruminating about the past. Being present and mindful is crucial in having real fun and enjoying the various benefits of engaging in behavioral activation. Choose suitable activities, be present and have lots of fun.

- ***Go slow at first:*** You can hardly manage to fit in so many activities after you are used to sleeping most of the time. Be kind to yourself and take things slowly, enjoying one activity at a time before adding another. You need to realize that the anxiety and depression will not wear off immediately. Take things slowly, and build your motivation, then move ahead.

- ***Take note of and reward progress:*** The day you finally step into the gym after a long time, note it down somewhere and give yourself a reward for taking that first and bold step. Every time you make any progress, reward yourself as a form of motivation to keep going.

Chapter Summary

In this chapter, we have looked at how important having fun is in improving mental health. We learned that:

- You should start by scheduling activities that are fun for you and those that have added value.
- If you need any form of motivation to either get started or keep going, do not be afraid to ask for help from your support circle.
- Do not strain yourself. The objective is to have fun.

In the next chapter, you will learn another CBT technique that can help you in fighting anxiety, depression and intrusive thoughts brought about by the beliefs we so dearly hold. It is time to test the beliefs!

CHAPTER NINE

Technique 7 – Testing the Beliefs

When we hold onto a belief for so long, we tend to think it's true, actually we just know it is a valid belief. These beliefs can occupy a huge part of our lives and shape the way we live our lives and relate to others. While having beliefs is a good thing and can help anchor us within life, they should not affect our daily lives, work and trouble us socially. If you are not living your best life because of beliefs, then it may be time to check if they are true and if they are worth the disruption to your life.

One of the most powerful tools available in CBT is behavioral experiments. The experiments are simply planned activities that aim to test the validity of those beliefs that you have. During this exercise, information is collected then used in testing your beliefs about yourself, others and the world. The method can also be used to test new and adaptive beliefs. You can think of behavioral experiments much like the scientific studies that prove a certain element is either as you make it to be or not.

The value of testing beliefs is that you are involved in the process and thus are not simply being told of the results. You gather the information and test the belief so its validity is clear to you without a doubt. You are, therefore, able to shed off some of the useless and inhibiting beliefs and replace those with positive beliefs.

Types of Behavioral Experiments

There are different ways you can test those beliefs that you hold based on the purpose. Some of these include:

1. *Surveys:* They can provide you with information on the belief you are testing. The method is helpful when you have a belief about what others think. For example, one belief could be that you believe that people will not like you if they know you suffer from anxiety.

2. *Experiential exercises:* They allow you to put specific beliefs to the test. For example, "If I exercise, I will pass out." You can engage in some exercise to see if it is true.

3. *Hypothesis testing:* This can be designed in a way that allows you to not only collect infor-

mation but also use it in the testing of the validity of your beliefs, predictions and thoughts. Hypothesis testing may involve:

- *Hypothesis A Testing:* Tests an existing and potentially unhelpful belief. For example, you may think that by exercising, you will pass out.

- *Hypothesis B Testing:* Tests a new belief. For instance, you may decide to embrace saying no. Try saying no when you're uncomfortable with something, then observe the results.

- *Hypothesis A vs. Hypothesis B:* This is a test between the original and the newly constructed belief to find out which one is better. For example, A could be, "Saying yes earns me more friends and respect," vs. B, "Saying no when I'm uncomfortable and being assertive earns me respect." You therefore test the two to see which one gives you the desired results, then adopt it.

4. **Direct observation:** Sometimes you may have a belief that you are not comfortable testing yourself. For example, you may believe that people do not care about others and, if anything

were to happen to you in the streets, people would pass right by you without offering help. If the fear is deeply set, you may find it difficult to test it. You can have someone else test it for you and you observe. For instance, your friend can pretend to collapse on the street as you observe how many people, if any, come to his aid.

5. ***Gathering information:*** There are many sources of information in today's world. The Internet, for instance, is full of information that you can use to prove or disprove your belief. For example, if you believe that the snowcaps will all melt and wash out the land all around causing massive deaths, it could help to research more on snowcaps and even watch how intense the melting process is and how many people are affected each year by the same. Information is power.

6. ***Discovery experiments:*** There are times when you can hold a feared belief so much that you just know if you do that, things will not be OK, but you cannot even explain how they will be. For example, you may believe that if you step out of the house after seven in the evening, something bad will happen, but you do not know what or why. You are not certain about

what to test here. With support, you can step out and take an evening walk to see what happens.

How to carry out a Behavioral Experiment

a) Identification of target cognition

You need to identify the target cognition as precisely as possible, including assessing how strongly you believe in this. You can use the 'If...then' formula. "If I exercise, then I will pass out."

Also, identify the safety behaviors you have put in place. For example, one such behavior could be that you always wear a reflector jacket when crossing the road. While you are here, also think through what you think would happen if you did not wear that reflector jacket.

Rate how deep your conviction is on a scale of 0-10, with 10 being that you're absolutely sure.

Now that you know what you are dealing with, we can move to the next step.

b) Design the Experiment

Depending on the belief, determine what will be the best way to test it, bearing in mind your readiness, safety and any other practicalities. You may also need to think of the occurrence of any other problems during the experiment. You should also check whether you are prepared to forego some of the safety behaviors for the success of the experiment.

Designing an experiment may take much mental effort, especially on the need to step out of your comfort zone. You may want to have another person help you in this phase. A therapist is a good choice.

Go ahead and undertake the experiment with an open mind.

c) *Outcome and Learning*

After the experiment, you need to take time to make meaning of what happened, as well as the data that you may have collected. Ask yourself, "What happened?" "What have you learned?" "Is there any change to your belief?" "Have you learned anything about yourself?" "Is there a better way of looking at things?" "Does the outcome support your original belief?" "Are there any contradictions?" "What are the implications of the test?" "Does it affect your daily life?"

d) *Way forward*

Take time to reflect on the outcome as well as what you have learned, then design a way forward. Some of the questions you can ask yourself include: "What have you learned from the experiment that can be replicated in other situations?" "What other experiments can you do?" "What do you need to do to maintain what you have learned?" "Have you developed a new perspective, and can it be tested?" "How do you put what you learned into practice?" "What else should you test?"

The purpose of testing these beliefs is to break any negative ones that you may be holding on to and, hence, free you from them. You can then enjoy life without unnecessary worries.

Chapter Summary

In this chapter, we have looked at how you can improve your mental health by testing those beliefs that seem to be disruptive to your life. We have learned that:

There are different methods that you can use to test your beliefs, such as discovery experiments, surveys, hypothesis testing and direct observation.

- Similar to a true scientist, you need to be acutely aware of what belief you are testing.
- You also need to ensure that you think through the testing process, including what could go wrong and the necessary safety measures.
- After results, it is important to review and reflect, including the lessons learned.
- You also have to incorporate the lessons into your life, otherwise what was the purpose of testing the belief in the first place?

In the next chapter, you will learn another CBT technique that can help you in fighting anxiety and intrusive thoughts through role-play.

CHAPTER TEN

Technique 8 – Role-Playing

Another technique that is useful in alleviating mental illnesses and offering you a happier easier life is role-playing. Sometimes you may become so anxious about an event that you find yourself panicking and unable to focus. You may be so anxious and stressed that you dread waking up in the morning. Other times, you may have a fear of something that is so bad that it affects your everyday life. At such time, you can benefit from a CBT technique called role-playing.

Role-playing helps you to develop a deep understanding or change within yourself. With this technique, you get an opportunity to perform certain behavior or act in a controlled, safe and risk-free environment. When role-playing, you can reenact yourself, another person, situation or circumstance, including your reactions. You can then get feedback either from a group, if you are working with a group, or a therapist or another individual.

Role-play mainly occurs in the present. You have to put yourself in the situation and reenact it as if it is happening now. Here, you do not work with either the future or the present, but just the present. Role-playing may be challenging as you start, as it requires you to fit into a certain role. You can start by reenacting the scenes that are easy, then move on to more complex ones.

How to Implement Role-Playing

Elements of Role Playing

As a prerequisite to role-playing, you need to understand the four main elements.

1. *The Encounter:* You need to be able to understand other people's perspective, as you may be required to play them in a certain situation.
2. *The Stage:* Refers to the space usually filled with simple props that provide a realistic experience.
3. *The Soliloquy:* As the name suggests, it is a speech in which you express your private thoughts, as well as the associated feelings. You are likely to come across your irrational beliefs here.
4. *Doubling:* Can really help you to have increased awareness, and it occurs when another

person stands behind you when you are reenacting a scene and helps to express any thoughts and feelings that you do not express.

Phases of Role Playing

Knowing these elements sets you up for role-playing. There is, however, more that you should learn. There are phases that you should go through when role-playing. These are:

- *Situation identification:* You have to correctly identify the situation to be reenacted as clearly as possible so that you know what you are dealing with and the potential outcomes.

- *The details:* The more detailed the situation is, the better the role-play can be and the better the results. Include all the necessary details. If it is in a coffee shop, consider even other patrons and what to order. Having tea or wine may contribute differently to the situation.

- *Warm-up phase:* Much like traditional acting, you need to connect with the situation and think through the emotions you will need in order to be able to reenact. You may choose to warm up either physically by doing a run-through of the situation or by doing so mentally. Ensure you are in the right frame of mind before beginning role-playing.

- *Action phase:* Here, you go over the details of the situation with the rest of the group, if in a group session or with the therapist, or even a friend. You also set the scene, paying attention to making it as realistic as possible and not using your imagination. You then reenact the situation, practically moving from your role to that of any other person in the situation. You have to ensure you are as practical and as realistic as possible. Having someone else there helps to ensure that you do not project your imagined worries or emotions.

- *Sharing and analysis:* The next phase involves sharing the lessons learned during the role-play. You can think of it as a reflective phase that looks back at the role-play and processes what happened.

- *Reenactment:* You can now repeat the exercise, paying attention to targeted behavior until you feel confident. For example, if you are role-playing a social situation and learning how to behave in such a manner that you are not overly anxious or a misfit, you can continually practice until you are confident and can socially fit in without many challenges.

- *Follow-up:* You need to regularly keep tabs on your progress. If you are handling the social scene much better, note that so you can celebrate the wins while working on the weaknesses.

Variations in Role Playing

There are different variations of role-play that you can use. Some of them include:

- *Behavioral rehearsal:* This involves rewarding and reinforcing the target behavior when you perform it. If you perform as expected without having negative behavior, you get a reward from a friend or even your therapist. You can even award yourself. The behavior is then reinforced through this method.
- *The mirror technique:* Works well in group-therapy sessions. Here, if you are reenacting a scene and critical behavior occurs, you have to take a seat. Someone else now comes in to take your place and reenacts the scene, usually exaggeratedly. You watch and can then evaluate his response, noting his mistakes. You can then

agree on a better way of responding for you to practice.

- *The Gestalt variation:* The method is mainly used by Gestalt therapists and makes use of two chairs standing in for other people. The chairs stand for you and anyone else you have an issue with, therefore their logic and desire. Your work is to sit in one chair and speak from the chair's (person's) point of view, expressing his thoughts and feelings.
- *Costume role-playing:* Works well with children and simply involves wearing different costumes during different roles. You, therefore, are keenly aware of who you are during the role-playing.

Benefits of Role Playing

We role-play often in our lives even when we do not have any phobias or anxiety issues to deal with. When you have a big interview, you may find yourself reenacting the scene in your head and practicing your responses. You may also stand in front of the mirror and practice asking that girl out on a date or how to react when you meet an important person. From these examples, you can tell that you are likely to be role-playing when nervous or anxious about something.

Role-playing is helpful in making you more confident when facing a certain situation, which in turn reduces the associated stress and anxiety. Since you have prepared for all scenarios, you feel able to deal with the situation.

Additionally, role-playing helps you to tackle both difficult and unfamiliar topics, as well as have emotionally difficult conversations, especially in conflict resolution. By reenacting the situation, you get a chance to address the issues before facing the actual situations. You are therefore better prepared for whichever direction the situation may take and the different ways they may respond. Since they do not catch you off guard, you can handle the situation well. Moreover, by going through the situation beforehand, you become aware of which responses can be counter-productive so you can avoid them.

Another benefit of role-playing is that it helps you get in touch with your feelings and thoughts about a situation in a way that helps you to clearly assess it without hiding your true feelings. You also get a clear view of how others feel about the situation and, hence, know how to approach things.

Role-playing also builds empathy and helps to improve communication skills, as well as sensitivity to the feelings and thoughts of others. Since you are not in denial, and you have insights into how the other person feels and what their perspective is, you are in a better position to communicate effectively and resolve any existing conflicts.

Aside from phobias, role-playing is an important technique in treating anxiety by preparing you for the world outside. The good news is that, if you are honest with yourself, you can role-play any situation and be better placed to handle whatever life throws at you.

Don't Shy Away

An interesting fact about role-playing is that it can feel stupid. Yes, you feel stupid standing in front of the mirror in your bedroom. Now, imagine having to reenact a scene among other people? The start is not easy, and you may need encouragement to continue, but you will be glad you did.

I role-play a lot. Every time I have a big event or a potentially difficult situation that I have to face, I role-play. From the exercise, I emerge strong and confident knowing that I have covered many of the bases, and I am ready for however the situation plays out.

Role-playing also calls for you to be very honest. Speaking or acknowledging our inner thoughts is no small feat, but it is something you have to do. You have to look within and not edit the thoughts and feelings. You also have to wear the other party's shoes and walk in them, acknowledging where the shoe pinches even when you know you have caused the pinch. In these times, it is recommended that you have a support system or join a group therapy where you can have someone point out those emotions that you may not feel confident enough to bring out. My time in therapy has taught me that honesty, particularly being honest with yourself, is a key component of the healing process.

Take time to role-play, whether alone or with others. You will realize that you grow mentally and emotionally stronger, empathize more, communicate better and become more confident.

Chapter Summary

In this chapter, we have looked at role-playing and its role in reducing anxiety, symptoms of depression and equipping you with confidence to go through life. We have learned that:

- Role-playing involves reenacting a scene or a situation, so you can look deeply into your feelings and thoughts.
- Role-playing always happens at the present.
- Through this technique, you are able to put yourself in another person's shoes and thus better understand him/her.
- It equips you with confidence to handle situations since you know what to expect.

In the next chapter, you will learn another CBT technique that can help you stop being overwhelmed by tasks by simply breaking them down.

CHAPTER ELEVEN

Technique 9 – Simply Break It Down

Have you ever dreaded the day ahead even before you embark on it? It could be that you have tasks that feel overwhelming, which stresses you out, makes you feel small, incompetent and unworthy? The truth is that we all feel overwhelmed at some point, but when it wears you down so much you begin to feel dysfunctional, then it is time to address this concern.

Some people have a difficult time completing a task. They may lack the necessary skills or are not familiar with it. Occasionally, the task may feel overwhelming and hard to do, resulting in stress, anxiety and a foul mood. If you are finding it difficult to complete tasks or reach your goals, do not despair; there is hope and treatment for you through successive approximation.

In simple terms, successive approximation is a CBT technique that calls for you to break down your tasks so they become easier to manage, and you can then work toward completing your goals. Instead of taking up the entire project or task, split it into smaller and easily manageable tasks that build up to get the whole project done. If you have anxieties that make it difficult for you to undertake any of the tasks that you need to, you can employ successive approximations.

Parts of Successive Approximations

In most parts, successive approximation is a simple yet effective technique that you can use at home to get things going while reducing the associated stress and anxiety. However, there are steps that you can follow to ease the process. After the initial step, you can do the other steps not in any particular order.

- ***Identify the task at hand:*** You have to be clear on what you want to do and achieve. Ensure that you know exactly what the task entails, including the details, so you do not leave anything undone. You do not want to complete the task only to find that there are some aspects not done.

- ***Setting subgoals:*** You want to modify your non-functional behavior into the desired behavior by successive approximations. Here, you break down the main task into smaller tasks that you can tick off as you go. Think of it as a staircase and you have to go up one step at a time to the next. For example, you may want to paint your exterior window frames, but are afraid of climbing up the ladder. The fear may be valid after falling down and breaking a leg four years ago. Since then, you have not been up a ladder, yet now you need to use one. Set your subgoals to be something like climbing up a step higher each day.

- ***Put the tasks in a chronological order:*** After you have split up the tasks into smaller ones, it is important that you arrange them in chronological order, so you are aware of what you need to do next and don't skip any important subtasks. For example, if you are going out for a work party and dread the social interaction, you can arrange to pack your bag, choose an outfit, iron your clothes, take a shower, put on your clothes, call a cab and grab your bag, among the other items you need to go out. Since you are nervous, chances of forgetting something are high. You do not want to arrive at the party after all the effort only to realize that you did not comb your hair. You will instantly feel like a loser, the same thoughts that we are working at avoiding.

- ***Identify triggers:*** With a good plan in place, you do not want the kind of surprises that neutralize all the hard work. You need to identify those triggers that will make you bail out on the task or those that demoralize you so they can be managed. For example, if seeing bandages will cause you to not attempt climbing the ladder, avoid them at all costs. If the triggers are in your head or among your friends, you want to stay away from that friend for that period.

- *Identify the sensitive aspects:* In most of these situations, you will realize that there are some sensitive aspects of which you should be aware. For example, you may find that some of the sensitive aspects when going for a party include your getting dressed, your ability to socialize and the menu. Knowing this will ensure that you are well-prepared to deal with them. You can opt to ask for professional help when choosing your outfit and settle for one that does not attract much attention. You can also role-play as you prepare for the party and ask about the menu in advance to make mental choices of what to have.

- *Commit:* You can't make much progress without making any commitment to the process. You have to ensure that you are willing to go through the subtasks to ensure that the entire process is done, then you can claim victory.

Steps for Successive Approximation Technique

1. *Find the starting place:* When facing a task—no matter how overwhelming—you will realize that it is not all bleak. There are parts of it that you can do without raising your anxiety level. For you to find the starting point for successive approximation, you have to find where your anxiety levels begin to go up. For example, if you are to climb the ladder and find out that even the sight of the ladder gets you very anxious, then that becomes your starting point. However, if you can climb the first two steps without feeling anxious, then the third step becomes your starting point.

2. *Withdraw when anxiety begins:* Once you know where to start, gather your courage and begin the journey. However, once your anxiety begins, withdraw immediately and head back to the comfort zone. If the first two steps on the ladder are comfortable for you to take, but you experience mild anxiety as soon as one foot finds the next step, you need to step back to where you feel safe. Take some time to take a breath and relax. This would be a good time to practice some of those breathing exercises before trying again when you feel ready to do so.

3. *Overcoming:* As you continue to practice and keep doing the subtasks one a time, you will feel better as you see progress. You will also gain more confidence to keep going through the list of tasks and ultimately achieve your purpose. Once you have achieved the first task, you will realize that you can keep repeating and even enjoying doing it. Take time to appreciate the progress and reward yourself for learning a new behavior.

The beauty of breaking down the tasks is that it simplifies each task and reduces any undue pressure that you may be under. You are likely to do much more than you have done in years when you apply successive approximation.

As you engage in this exercise, it is important that you are kind to yourself, allowing time for you to gain courage to keep going. Don't expect that it will instantaneously work, enabling you to do so much, you may need to take the time to go through the subtasks. Therefore, while you may have a target to achieve, save yourself the extra pressure that comes with strict deadlines. If you are able to accomplish a subtask, pat yourself on the back.

Chapter Summary

In this chapter, we have looked at how simpler life and tasks can be if we break them down. Similar to how we cut our food into bite-sized chunks, it is important to also break down our tasks, especially those that seem overwhelming and difficult, into subtasks, then implement them one by one. We have also learned that:

- We should only undertake a task when we feel ready to do it. Piling on additional pressure will be counterproductive.
- Arrange the subtasks in chronological order where possible to avoid missing a task, which will be demoralizing.
- If you need help, ask for support. Some tasks take a lot of guts, especially in the face of past failure or hurt. Ask for support when you need it.
- Once you accomplish a task, take time to reward yourself, then keep practicing.

In the next chapter, you will learn another CBT technique, which can help to keep you in the present and prevent your thoughts from wandering into volatile zones, called mindfulness.

CHAPTER TWELVE

Technique 10 – Mindfulness

Our minds ideally should concentrate on the task at hand except that they occasionally veer off and bring in everyone and everything they meet on the way. Have you ever been working on a project then your mind goes fishing for what would possibly go wrong or what someone thinks of you or the failures that came with the last project? You find yourself having moved from the task at hand to concentrating on those things that the mind brought in, yet you know they will cause you stress, anxiety and self-doubt. You can benefit from a CBT technique, called Mindfulness-Based Cognitive Therapy (MBCT).

What is MBCT?

MBCT is a technique that works by combining mindfulness strategies with cognitive behavioral techniques in helping you understand and manage your emotions and thoughts better and get reprieve from any distressing feelings. The technique works well for a variety of mental illnesses.

During psychotherapy, you combine cognitive therapy, mindfulness and meditation. Mindfulness refers to a state of focusing on being acutely aware of what you are feeling and sensing presently without judgment or interruption. Throughout the process, you will learn to recognize and understand your feelings and thought patterns, then you can create new and more effective ones.

In most cases, MBCT works as a group intervention lasting up to eight weeks, and, I must say, the time is worth it. You are required to have a two-hour weekly course and a day-long class sometime after the fifth week. While some of the learning happens in the session, most of the practice happens outside the sessions. You will have to do some homework that may include listening to guided meditations and cultivating mindfulness in your activities by applying the MBCT skills. You also get to learn the three-minute breathing space.

Three-Minute Breathing Space

Usually, this is a quick exercise that is done in three steps:

1. In the first minute, you ask yourself, "How am I doing right now?" while observing your experience and trying to find the right words for those thoughts, sensations and feelings.
2. During the second minute you focus on breath.
3. You spend the last minute expanding your attention from just your breath to the physical sensations and their effect on your body.

How does it work?

Through MBCT, you can tackle those intrusive thoughts by learning to use mindfulness mediation in disrupting the processes that often trigger those thoughts and emotions. Allowing such thoughts to happen leads to low mood, weariness, sluggishness, and negative thoughts taking over and that makes you anxious and depressed. Worse is that even after such an episode, there are chances that you may feel blue, and small other things, like fatigue, can easily trigger another episode.

In this technique, you learn to recognize that you are a separate entity from your mood and thought, giving you a sense of being. Understanding that your thoughts and emotions do not define you can help you allow you to be liberated from negative thought patterns that may be playing on repeat mode in your head.

You begin to appreciate your thoughts and emotions but also know that they are separate from you and although they can both exist simultaneously, they do not have to lead you where they please. You can go in the opposite direction—into the land of positivity—which disarms the negative ones. You are the one who matters, the one who decides what to give power to.

You also learn various skills in MBCT that help you in combating those low, blue and depressive thoughts and symptoms as they arise. Learning MBCT skills helps you to have your own army and strategies that you can refer to when you feel like the mental battlefield is getting hot or overwhelming. Besides, knowing that you are prepared for such times of intrusive thoughts, anxiety and depression gives you confidence in your ability to deal with them, making you approach things from a winner's perspective.

Benefits of MBCT

There are many benefits of MBCT. Some of them include:

- Helps you discover your own mood and thought patterns.
- Helps you learn how to focus on the present and enjoy the small pleasures of life.

- Teaches you how to stop the downward spiral that comes with painful memories and bad moods.
- Learning how to shift to a balanced and non-judgmental mental state.
- Improved physical health, since most of the techniques include some form of exercise.
- Reduced stress that comes with focusing on the present and soothing exercises, like yoga.
- Improved concentration on tasks, increasing your chances of succeeding.
- Improved overall mood.
- Better ability to face the challenges of life.

MBCT Techniques

Other MBCT techniques include:

1. Body Scan

Earlier on, we touched on the body scan. Here, you lie on your back with palms up and feet slightly apart or you sit comfortably on a chair with your feet on the floor. You have to stay very still during this exercise and only move deliberately, fully aware if you need to adjust your position.

Next, with the help of the facilitator, you bring awareness to your breath, taking note of the rhythm of inhaling and exhaling. Now, move attention to your body, take in everything about it, including how it feels, the clothing texture, temperature, contours of the surface you are lying on, and the entire environment. Once you have mastered that, focus your attention on any part of the body that is feeling light, heavy, sore or even tingly. Move any parts where you feel no sensation.

Scan the entire body, starting from the toes, paying attention to how each body part feels. Move up to the rest of the foot, up the legs and all the way to the top of the head. Once you finish scanning every bit of your body, gently bring back awareness to the room where you are, opening your eyes slowly and moving to a comfortable sitting position.

2. Mindful Stretching

You have to bring in mindfulness to your situations, and one way of doing so is incorporating it into your stretching. Before you rush to exercise, take time to have some mindful stretching, which prepares both your body and mind for the upcoming physical exertion. Besides, mindful stretching can help increase your sense of balance and awareness. Below are some mindful-stretching options you can try.

- **Pandiculation:** Means a fairly simple stretch. All you have to do is place your palms on your shoulders, raise your elbows to the height of the shoulders, then open your mouth to let out a satisfying yawn.

- **Yoga poses:** The four main ones are:

  1. *Side-to-side neck stretch:* Sit and gently use your hand to pull the neck from side to side.

  2. *Gomukhasana:* Open your chest as you extend the triceps and shoulders while sitting cross-legged or kneeling.

  3. *Pigeon pose:* Your hips should be on the floor with one leg in front of you and perpendicular to the mat. The other leg stays straight out behind you.

  4. *The scorpion:* Start by lying flat with your arms stretched out to the side. Lift your right foot high, keeping your sole straight up to the ceiling before lifting the right hip too. Now, move the lifted foot to the outside of the other leg, while keeping your arms and chest on the floor. You can then switch legs.

3. **Mindful Showering**

When you are just beginning, this is a good place to start, incorporating mindfulness in your daily activities. Give attention to the water temperature as it touches your body, feeling the spray, smell of the soap and the sensation of the lathered soap. If your mind begins to wander, as is common, steer it back to the present by focusing on what you are hearing, feeling, seeing and smelling.

4. Mindful Eating

Similarly, this involves giving all your attention to what you are eating. It helps if you can turn off things, like the TV, phone or radio, that are disruptive, so you can focus just on eating. Feel the texture of the food, concentrate on the aroma and the taste.

5. Mindfully Brushing Teeth

Don't laugh. Keeping in the present is important, and what better way to do so than focusing on the everyday activities that you undertake, especially brushing your teeth? Focus your attention on the strokes of the brush, their movement and feel on your teeth and gums. Give attention to the taste of the toothpaste and how it feels in your mouth.

In essence, you can incorporate mindfulness into all areas of life and your daily activities. By doing so, you learn to focus on the present, filter your thoughts to what you want then to be and, hence, exercise control over your thoughts and emotions. The main idea with mindfulness is not to change what you are doing but rather to pay attention and notice what you are doing. Gone will be the days you drove home and can't remember taking the last three turns or eating and not remembering the food's taste.

Learning to incorporate mindfulness in my life has been helpful in keeping me in the present, helping me appreciate the coffee, the sunshine, the flowers and all the simple beautiful things that life has to offer. I practice mindfulness so much in my daily life that it has become a part of me. When I feel those intrusive thoughts and anxiety about issues creeping in, I switch them off through mindfulness. I no longer go for coffee with a friend and spend the time worrying about work or things I haven't done. No, I sit there in the present, engage in the conversation, savor the coffee and the activities around the coffee shop. After that, I am glad I went out. I get to laugh, enjoy some good company and generally feel good. You should try it.

Chapter Summary

In this chapter, we have looked at how you can use mindfulness to gain control of your emotions and feelings, as well as stay in the present moment. We have seen how helpful this technique can be in alleviating symptoms of depression, reducing stress and anxiety, pushing away intrusive thoughts. We have also learned that:

- You can incorporate mindfulness in your day-to-day activities, like eating, breathing and walking.
- You can also practice mindful stretching, body scan and yoga, among others, to help you to refocus and shed the negative thoughts and emotions.
- MBCT helps you to be able to face the challenges of life by providing you with useful techniques that you can follow to fight off negative emotions and incorporate positive ones.

CHAPTER THIRTEEN

Technique 11 – Play the Entire Script

You probably know those thoughts that refuse to leave, at least not without a fight. The kind that sticks around long enough to convince you that they are legit, and you should be prepared for the worst. The kind that slowly creep in your head and, before long, they are deteriorating. For example, you ask a colleague to have coffee with you, and he agrees. Then the thought strikes, "He won't show up. He doesn't even like working with me. Leaves me alone to have coffee." Before long, the thought has graduated to, "Nobody even likes working with me. I am a horrible person. Nobody loves me." Soon, you find yourself in a foul mood, feeling stressed, anxious and with many other intrusive thoughts flying in and out as they please.

When you are catastrophizing, you see only the possibility of a disaster happening, even when there are no indications, or you take any small sign to indicate that bad things will happen. You also tend to jump to conclusions without evidence. If you are one of these people that suffer from anxiety and fear and only imagine the worst-case scenario, then you need a CBT technique that simply tells you to play the script to the end. There is no hurry and no need to jump to conclusions.

Through decatastrophizing or playing the entire script, you can learn to think differently when faced with emotional situations, offer emotional regulation and generally reduce anxiety and catastrophic thinking.

Important Tips

- ***Take a step back:*** Instead of focusing on the worst-case scenario, take a step back and see how similar situations have previously played out.

- ***Recognize that catastrophizing is negative:*** You may take catastrophizing as a way of protecting yourself from danger and problems. While, in some cases, anxiety does that, there is nothing positive about catastrophizing. You have to focus and respond to the situation on the ground, not build up scenarios in your head.

- ***Recognize those negative thoughts:*** A simple way of doing this is by asking yourself if your thoughts are appropriate and realistic as per the situation.

- ***Bring out the evidence:*** Some catastrophic thoughts can be relentless, so bring out the evidence. You can ask yourself based on experience the likelihood of your worry becoming true. For example, if someone doesn't want to have coffee with another, they decline. Acceptance means willingness.

- ***Maintain perspective:*** You have to focus on the reality and maintain that perspective. Ask yourself how you will feel in a week's time or more, depending on the situation.

- ***Imagine and visualize:*** Looking ahead is important. Imagine having that coffee with that colleague and the conversation. You can also detach yourself from the situation and imagine offering advice to a friend and looking back at this in the future after the event has happened. We tend to be kinder to others, and so it helps if you give your place to someone else, then you can see things more clearly.

Steps in Decatastrophizing

1. **Generate Alternative Explanations**

Instead of only focusing on the worst-case scenario, give it some siblings to play with. Ideally, you should develop three scenarios: the worst-case scenario, the best-case scenario, and then the most-likely scenario.

You already have the worst-case scenario that your mind has labored tirelessly over, so it is time to develop the best-case scenario. Put effort in making it as humorous, happy, lavish, perfect, light and fun as you possibly can. It should be a complete opposite of the worst-case scenario.

For the most-likely scenario, think as realistically as you can, considering the best-case and the worst-case scenario. You can use previous experience to make up this scenario.

You will realize that you are already feeling better since you have allowed yourself to see other possibilities.

2. Assess Probabilities

Look at those scenarios in earnest and assess the probability of their actually happening. You will realize that the best-case scenario and the worst-case scenario both have a low probability of coming true, usually less than 5%. The highest probability goes to the most-likely scenario. Life is usually not that extreme.

3. Develop a Coping Strategy

Since you may not be fully convinced that the worst-case scenario will not happen and justifiably so, there is still a 5% probability. You may feel better if you have a coping strategy to deal with the unlikely occurrence of the worst-case scenario. Alternatively, you can skip this step.

Come up with measures to implement if the worst-case situation occurs. Being prepared will reduce stress and anxiety and stop those thoughts from haunting you.

Over time, you can break the habit of catastrophizing simply by allowing the script to run till the end without jumping to conclusions. Go for the coffee date and see how it goes, instead of making up thousands of scenarios and reasons why it will be a disaster. It could be what you needed to unwind, and you could end up with great insights that make your work better.

Chapter Summary

In this chapter, you have learned about another CBT technique, called playing the entire script. In particular, you have learned that:

- You do not need to jump to conclusions about the situation. Instead of thinking of the worst-case scenario, let the entire script play out.
- Developing a coping strategy could help those who cannot seem to find peace by preparing them for its unlikely occurrence.
- Catastrophizing is negative.

FINAL WORDS

The world of mental illnesses can be dark, gloomy and lonely. You may feel like you do not want to go on with life, especially when dealing daily with stress, anxiety, depression and intrusive thoughts. However, it is time to be courageous and resolve to get better. I did it. I started on the journey to health, wellness, peace and calm, albeit reluctantly. Here I am today: whole, energized, healthy and glowing with inner peace.

As we have seen in this book, there are some easy CBT techniques that we can use to make our lives better. Of course, it is important to see a therapist or a mental-health professional who will do an assessment and provide a diagnosis of what ails you, enabling you to take action. While there are different treatment methods, I find that Cognitive Behavioral Therapy works the best. In addition to being very effective, you can complete it in a short time, you can practice most of the techniques at home, and you can work by refocusing your thoughts, emotions and behavior in a manner that gets rid of the negative ones and welcomes positivity.

The first step in addressing mental-health disorders is to ensure safety. You may have had the thought of how liberating it would be to check out of this world and leave all the suffering and hopelessness behind. You are not alone, I attempted to do so. But you do not have to. Instead, focus on creating a safety plan. If you don't do anything else, create a safety plan. You will be able to know when things are spiraling out of control and know what to do about it. Having this plan does not make you vulnerable, no, it makes you prepared for the extremely dark days. You are less likely to give in to those harmful thoughts when you have a plan and follow it.

We have looked at 11 techniques that you can use either at home or in therapy with a qualified mental-health professional. If you look keenly at these techniques, you will notice that they are simple and easy to apply. You can exercise mindfulness in your daily activities, you can role-play in front of your mirror and you can easily subdivide overwhelming tasks even in the comfort of your home or in traffic. There are also many ways of taking the stress off and have some fun to keep the mood light and positivity up. You can have fun with your friends, laugh, play a game or any other activity that makes you feel good. You can also find ways to relax, like going for a massage, lighting candles, listening to smooth music or taking a walk.

For you to see the effectiveness of these techniques, it is important that you are committed to the process.

You are not likely to see results in a day. Besides, the beginning is always the hardest. You will have to be willing to step out of your comfort zone and take action. If you choose to schedule activities that make you feel better, you have to follow through and attend those events. There is no wishing the negative thoughts away. You have to get up and work toward a better mental health. The good news is that it gets better with time. As you progress with whichever technique you choose, you will realize that it becomes a part of you. You will be mindful of eating in no time, you will embrace relaxation and fun. You will appreciate cognitive restructuring and note how easy you can identify a negative thought and immediately replace it with a positive one. Your mood will lift, you will laugh and love more. All the simple exercises will make your body strong and beautiful, while your mind will be a power to reckon with. No longer will you be hiding away in your blanket, afraid to draw the curtains and face a new day. Instead, you will wake up energized and ready to tackle whatever challenge the world throws at you, and it will. You will ooze of positivity and will look forward to a long, joyful and successful life.

Choose techniques that work with whatever shortcomings that you may have or use a combination of technique to cover a large base. If you find that a technique is not working effectively for you, don't struggle. Adopt another one. CBT works at reducing your anxiety, stress and intrusive thoughts, not increasing them. Take things easy, but be eager to learn, grow and feel better. Remember that you are making all the effort for your own good, to have a quality life and enjoy it with those around you.

Do not allow mental illnesses to intimidate you, you can overcome through Cognitive Behavioral Therapy. There is hope for a fuller better life!

"Change your thoughts and you will change your world."
— Anonymous

You've finally found it!

The one place for REAL people seeking to finally answer the burning question that's plagued them all their life:

"Why am I such a f*ckwit, can't knuckle down and never can do anything with my life"

Everybody, no matter what station they are at in their life wants to do better. Nobody ever says " I wish I could do worse. I wish I could be paid less"

With that in mind, people are either moving ahead or they are floundering. The is no middle ground. And therein lies the opportunity.

Everything seems to be going ok. Good job, nice business, steady income, the bills are getting paid and home life is pretty good.

Yet you feel like you are the 24/7, 365-day hamster wheel. The harder you run, the faster it goes. You wish to break the cycle but it seems impossible. Your dream of the perfect job where you become the top dog, can control your time, take Wednesdays off for golf, never seems to come to fruition.

You've tried self-help stuff; books, courses, live events and so on. You get all pumped up at the event and then….flat. Your credit card bill comes in

PRELUDE

No B S Strategies To Stop F*cking Around In The Next 30 Days

*- Daily Principles For
Those Who Hate Self-Help*

"Hey, I never knew about your lifestyle changes so many years ago
„ I admire your decisions and commitment to the most precious things in life „ YOU & those you love and Finding your voice😊"

WHAT OTHERS ARE SAYING ABOUT GREG REED

Facebook Comments

"Sometimes self-reflection and allowing yourself not to conform or fit in gives you the freedom to find not only your voice but like-minded people. You allowed me to be myself during our time at the same company and befriended me which is something I've never forgotten and am so grateful for.

Enjoy your contentment and peace in who you are Greg, you deserve it. X"

"Thanks for your lift me up post was just what I needed to read today.... about to have a listen to that podcast.... have a great day ☺"

"Greg, I don't have to remind you that I have known you for some time, in saying that I have always admired you for your loyalty, motivation and inspiration you are one unique character and do not change my friend ☺"

"Mad respect for you Mate!"

Success awaits you!

G N Reed

PS If you liked this short book please leave me a review on the site you bought the book from. I'd appreciate that. Book publishers and store owners love it too.

for you here, waded through the garbage, invested thousands and condensed the best 'how to' tips into this book. I don't have a PhD in psychology but I do possess a MCS – Master of Common Sense. I've made it to 62; not bad!

I've discovered the journey on 'how to' be successful at almost anything follows a similar pattern. Identifying this pattern, understanding its components and applying these 'how to' strategies that I'll reveal, can lead you to a better life.

In this book I'll show you how in 30 days you can stop f*cking around and improve your life.

Each step will move you through your day creating a better outcome than yesterday.

I cover a lot of ground in a very short book. This is deliberate. My book is 'NO B. S., Kick Butt, Take No Prisoner' (love this from Dan Kennedy) crammed with strategies. I hate padding. I'm busy and so are you.

BUT…..

Yes, there is a 'but'. Your better life will only improve if after you read my tips, **you take action.** My strategies work but you must apply them!

Good luck on your improvement journey.

ABOUT THE AUTHOR

My name is Greg Reed and I am a no B.S, take no prisoners, kick butt kind of guy. I don't have an original thought in my head. Everything I regurgitate has been 'stolen' through reading, listening and watching over the past sixty + years. I'm now 62 with a crushing desire to pontificate my views on life.

Simply put, it's my consumption of life. There are no new ideas. Just old ideas delivered differently.

The purpose of this books is to show how through continuous personal development, you can live a better life. <u>This book is short, sharp and to the point.</u>

It is designed for busy people wanting to get to the next level but don't want to waste time sifting through the B.S. I have discovered the best way to make these changes in your life: <u>improve one thing at a time</u>.

Like you, I've been on the journey of self-improvement all my life. I've done the heavy lifting

Day 15	Stop Being a People Pleaser............................75
Day 16	Have Fun...79
Day 17	Improvement Over Perfection.......................82
Day 18	Avoiding Toxic People....................................86
Day 19	Be Flexible...91
Day 20	Better Questions Get Better Answers.........94
Day 21	Choosing What's Right For You...................97
Day 22	Stop Over Thinking Stuff.............................101
Day 23	You're Never Too Old...................................105
Day 24	What's Your Reality?.....................................109
Day 25	Living With Purpose.....................................113
Day 26	When Your Body Speaks, Listen................119
Day 27	Don't Waste Your Potential.........................124
Day 28	The Unbreakable Must-Do's.......................128
Day 29	Unlearn Limiting Beliefs..............................133
Day 30	Get Your Priorities Right.............................136

The Last Word (s)..141

TABLE OF CONTENTS

About the Author 1

Prelude 7

Day 1   Motivation Is B.S. 13

Day 2   It's Not the Right Time 18

Day 3   Your Past Is Not Your Future 23

Day 4   What's The Lesson? 27

Day 5   Stop Shooting Yourself In The Foot 31

Day 6   Opportunity Doesn't Knock 36

Day 7   Don't Follow the Herd 41

Day 8   Don't Be a Quitter 44

Day 9   Overcoming Emotional Burnout 49

Day 10   Who the Heck Are You? 54

Day 11   Discover New Experiences 57

Day 12   Stop Trying to Change Others 61

Day 13   What Is Your Success? 65

Day 14   Suck It Up Precious 70

Copyright

Copyright © 2021 by Greg N Reed
Cover and internal design © Wood Duck Media

All rights reserved. No part of this book may be reproduced in any form or by any electronic or mechanical means including information storage and retrieval systems – except in the case of brief quotations in articles or reviews – without the permission in writing from its publisher, Greg N Reed.

All brand names and product names used in this book are trademarks, registered trademarks, or trade names of their respective holders. We are not associated with any product or vendor in this book.

Greg N Reed has asserted his right under the Copyright, Designs and Patents Act 1988 to be identified as the author of this work.

ISBN: 9780648460541

Wood Duck Media is committed to a sustainable future for our business, our readers and our planet. This book is made from Forest Stewardship Council certified paper.

www.WoodDuckMedia.com

WOOD DUCK MEDIA

STOP F*CKING AROUND

30 Daily Actionable Steps

By

Greg N Reed

www.ingramcontent.com/pod-product-compliance
Lightning Source LLC
Chambersburg PA
CBHW030111240426
43673CB00002B/39

and the 'Guru Mastermind' you attended last week for the 'discounted sum of $2500 is now screaming at you off the statement.

But that's ok. You got a photo with the 'legend' as part of your 'discounted V. I. P deal. At least it created a few likes on Facebook.

It's a confusing world out there. Even more so for the fully paid up person who continually f*cks around. The more you generally buy into the spinning vortex, the more overwhelmed you become.

Everybody is an 'advisor' telling you to do this and that and something else. It's hard to keep up, let alone improve.

I'm here to help you. To mute the noise, declutter your mind and to provide you with practical strategies to get you on track. These are not tactics or tips. They are seasonal. Strategies are tried and true and remain evergreen.

WHY I WROTE THIS BOOK

I'm here to offer radical but not new, challenging but not impossible, proven concepts that will test just about everything you've consumed to date is wrong.

I'm going to show you the trees over the forest, turn down the sound volume to create peace and restfulness and close your eyes on distracting media; especially social media.

If you get it you'll say to yourself 'why didn't I see this earlier'. Some of you may even give yourself a swift upper cut.

This 'change' will require work. You may be ridiculed by your family and friends. You maybe born into a family of f*ckwits. You'll have your back to the wall Sunny Jim. You'll need a steel spine to stay the course.

But if you can overcome the torment of being labelled a 'tosser', drop kick and loser' you'll end up in a happier place than the 'sheep following, card carrying, fully paid-up stress addict popping pills by the hour just to stay out of the but house'.

WHERE DID I 'STEAL' THESE IDEAS?

There are no new ideas, only ideas delivered in a different way. These strategies are not stolen. For me it's been a life long journey. No degrees, no PhD, just a disciple of consistency and an appetite to learn.

I discovered:

- You can have a mansion on the most exclusive beach and be mentally f*cked.
- You can run a global conglomerate and still be a basket case
- You can attend every Tony Robbins (nothing against Tony) seminar and sill be mentally 'broke'
- You can be the largest donator at your church but still worry about your next dollar
- You can have 100,000 Facebook followers screaming your name, but you really are a fraud. You live with imposter syndrome every day.

Here's your reality. Unless you wake up to yourself and stop being a f*ckwit you're going to continue to spiral out of control and the spend the rest of your life on a psychologist's sofa sprouting your woe-is-me story and burning your credit card beyond recognition.

IT'S TIME FOR A DIFFERENT VISION

As you read through this short book, you may feel you've heard this all before.

I hope you have. The ideas have been around for a long time. I'm here to present these strategies differently. Provide you with a reference point.

The book is deliberately short. You don't have time to read 'war and peace' and then go get a bachelor's degree to understand the whole damn thing. The sentences are short for a better reading experience, especially if you read this book off a tablet or iPhone.

I promise to:

- Take you beyond the 'pony show' and reveal thirty strategies that'll propel you on your improvement journey like never before
- In this book reduce your confusion, provide you with clarity, build your self-esteem and help you become the master of your own destiny.

Are you ready to break free? Let's get started.

This book can be read in any order. Come back to your favourite 'day' at any time. You are in charge!

DAY 1

MOTIVATION IS B.S.

Ooops I've probably just torched any chance of me getting an invite into the 'Motivational Guru's Inner Circle' Club. I dare say Tony Robbins won't be inviting me onto his private jet for a meeting to discuss a possible co-authored book and I could probably kiss good-bye any hook ups with Deepak Chopra or Oprah. But that's ok for now. Let me explain.

Motivation is such a temporary thing. You pay top dollar to attend a show by one of these gurus, maybe even buying the upsell to get backstage and have your photo taken with the motivational messiah.

It's worth the extra $799, right? Imagine what your friends will say when you change your profile pic on Facebook to include your new best tycoon pal. Give me a break!

Have you worked out yet why they are rich and you're not? Can you guess why? Stop buying photos! Nobody really believes that Richard Branson is your new, best buddy.

Am I sounding a bit cynical? Too right I am. Our psyche goes up and down. You attend a motivational speech and boom you are ready to take on the world.

Until you hit a brick wall or even less, stub your toe. Everybody goes up and down even your new bestie Richard Branson. <u>The trick is to stay focused.</u>

You have to keep going, even when you don't feel like it. Remember that New Year's Eve Resolution on how you were going to get up every morning and go for a 30-minute walk.

Well, if today is one of those days when you want to stay rugged up in bed because the temperature is a bit chilly, throw back the covers, slip into the active wear and head out the door. And guess what you'll be saying in thirty minutes from now "I feel better now".

Motivation is sometimes described as the state of a person's mind when they first start something new.

Like learning to play guitar. You imagine yourself as the next Hendrix (well a live Hendrix at least) or Clapton but when after a month you are still having difficulties moving your fingers from an A chord to an E, you place the Les Paul back on the stand to gather dust and justify the $2500 you spent on your maxed out credit card will be repaid one day.

<u>Motivation is so very unpredictable.</u>

If we give into its sweet seduction that everything is going to be good, we invite uncertainty into our lives.

Uncertainty in most people leads to some state of anxiety from a mild case of life is crap to let's book into rehab and sort this out. Trying to sort your shit out while relying on external things like motivation will lead to pain.

Put simply motivation is not enough to get things done.

Successful people adopt a more practical plan to getting things done.

Yes, you might see your Porsche driving, Italian suit wearing neighbour sitting ringside at a guru's seminar but if that son-of-a-gun is a ridgey didge, full blown, card carrying member of the 'success club', then he won't be relying on motivation to get the job done.

He'll have a practical plan to stay focused no matter what, to take consistent action and to keep going. Maybe that's how he got to sit ringside while you're down the back with the wannabes?

Perseverance is key to success.

Successful people know that in order to achieve something good, it will take time. Rome wasn't built in a day is their motto. And to achieve greatness, well it just takes a little longer.

Successful people make the commitment to make the change.

It's a non-negotiable thing. If you want to lose weight, you can't stop by Rosie's Bakery and knock back a cream donut for afternoon tea. Rosie is going to have to survive with one less customer.

But don't worry another junkie for sugar laded treats will soon replace you and Rosie will survive. And so will you in a healthier state.

Commitment turns those 'do I really have to' behaviours into fulltime ways to live.

You'll start noticing the difference and you'll be pleased with the end result.

Motivation is nice to get all warm and fuzzy but it's your commitment to put one foot in front of the other and keep going that really makes all the difference.

I hope Tony, Oprah or Deepak haven't banned me forever. Any front row tickets?

DAY 2

IT'S NOT THE RIGHT TIME

Here we go. Let's dish up a favourite "It's not the right time" response.

Your mates have asked you to come away for the weekend to watch the footy grand final. It's a $500 expense and once again you are short on the readies, 'the dough-ray-me', the 'Charles Ash' or for you non- Aussies, the cash.

Or ladies (and you were thinking this is a bloke's only disease), your girlfriends are having lunch in a swank riverside restaurant this Friday and even though the eye candy will be first class (or rich…..does it come any other way), the credit card is in melt down and hubby boo is over paying the bill.

Yes, you can just whip out the old faithful excuse but if you seem to be making this a regular thing, then perhaps you need to address it. And that means actually doing something about it.

Aaagh did I actually say that. Did I swear by using the most shocking two letter word in the English-speaking language; 'do'. Crikey. Breathe deep, in out, deep breaths. Yes, I'm going to give you another heart flutter. If you've been peddling the same shit for a lifetime, wake the f*ck up.

Mmmm that's better. I'm feeling better now. If I keep on saying this in this book, I think some medical insurance mob is going to come along and steal my line. Sorry another Aussie joke but members of Medibank Private Insurance will know what I mean.

Some people are waiting for some magical period in their life to come along and everything will be better. They are hoping a leprechaun fairy will appear on their shoulder and guide them through life, make things better, and to live a great life.

You know these people. They are looking skyward waiting for a vision. Let's not get religious here, but looking up to the heavens won't help you.

The 'it's not the right time' sayers believe they will know 'when it is the right time'. Well, they have to believe that otherwise if they don't their whole world crumbles and they drive to the top of the State bridge and jump. Or they get hit by a bus waiting for the right time and die anyway.

The sorry thing though is that a lot of people will keep on deluding themselves rather than taking a good solid look in the mirror and owning up to their own failures.

Sadly, there is only one person who believes them; it's themselves. Others may nod their heads, carry on as if they understand then scamper way and talk behind their friend's back.

There is no right time, Freddy. You have to make it the right time. You need to create the change by facing up to your responsibilities and taking action.

Sure, it can be tough. You may need to get a little uncomfortable. It may even hurt but you need to face it now for all those things you didn't do in the past.

For some that may mean forgoing expensive takeaway lunches and actually making lunch at home to take to work.

This simple thing will save you around $200/month which you can put towards your maxed out credit card or into a savings account for Christmas. I feel better now (I wish I would stop saying that, but it's not the right time).

Creating the shift to a better life has little to do with the 'right time' and more about the right you. Yes, it's a you thing.

It may be a fear thing, a mind thing or 'I'll get around to it' thing but it's definitely a thing we need to address or continue to miss out on the good stuff in life.

So, what's it to be. Another year doing the same old stuff waiting for the right time? You can talk about it, plan it, buy a course on goal setting or even sign up for a few seminars, but without action nothing will change.

Stop procrastinating. Face your fears which is often false evidence appearing real anyway and just do it!

And guess what you'll be saying once you've taken the action. "That wasn't so bad after all".

Make the right time now time.

DAY 3
YOUR PAST IS NOT YOUR FUTURE

Usually, this phrase is said with negative connotations. Unless it is your sole intention to lead a miserable life, then we need to do something about it.

It may not even be conscious. The 'I'm crap at dating girls' idea maybe some deep buried thought that was created way back in Year 5 when Sally Pendergast said no to you at the under 12's dance and is now totally determining how you approach women for a date. At forty-six Jack, we had better get this sorted. Read on.

Having negative thoughts from our past is not something that we should completely dismiss, we are human after all. But we can't let such thoughts totally run our lives either.

We need to learn from the past and move forward. Easier said than done I hear you naysayers scream at the page. Ok, ok let's keep cool. Grab a Pepsi, no better still a cold glass of water, and take a refreshing drink. (I just resisted saying 'I feel better now').

To make the change you'll need to grab a quiet place, think about what you want to do, and start taking action. Otherwise, your past will be like a dead weight you'll carry around forever.

You can't change the past. I once met a guy who lost a million dollars in a day trading on the share market. He lost his home, then his family. Every day he would ruminate on how terrible his life was, how dumb he was to have lost that much money and why nobody would stick by him in his 'hour' of need. Unfortunately, his hour lasted twenty-three years until he finally realized he had to let go.

There was only one thing that was making his life awful. It wasn't the loss of money. He was a smart guy applying dumb conversations to his subconscious. He was his own worst enemy. The crazy thing is that the problem didn't exist anymore. It was something that occurred in the past. The money was lost in the past.

But he held onto this thought with a vice-like grip. Everybody else had moved on including his ex-wife who married a millionaire. Maybe that kept him grumpy. It had become part of his identity and perhaps for that reason he could not give it up. That would equate to another loss in his eyes but one that he should forego.

To him the loss had meaning but to others it meant nothing. Sure, people could sympathize with him but without experiencing it themselves, they were merely conversations without any real feelings. Things, experiences and thoughts only have power we give them. If they are negative, we stop living in the now.

Now is the only place to live. We can't get back the past. It's gone, over, finished. We can't live in the future either. Things may or may not happen in the future.

Sure, we can plan for the future by eating well, performing well in our job, saving money for retirement or putting some balance into our life, but we don't have any guarantee that those things will come true.

Don't stay trapped in your history. You are robbing yourself of evolving and moving forward. Live in the now and let go your negative past and move on. There's a bright future in front of you if you embrace it.

DAY 4
WHAT'S THE LESSON?

Life throws up lessons every day. Are you seeing them or are you letting them slip by?

Lessons can be born out of success or failure. Too often we attribute lessons with failure but there are equally good lessons to be learned from success. But no matter which side of the fence the lesson falls, it depends on whether you are open to receiving that lesson.

For some failure is seen as the end of the road. To others seeing the failure, a lesson can be learned.

A mother experiences a break down in her marriage. She blames herself for not paying attention to her husband as being the reason as to why he had an affair with his 23-year-old personal assistant.

She questions whether her conversation at home became boring having not worked outside the house for the past ten years and therefore not contributing enough stimulating conversation.

There is no simple answer to her dilemma. Her husband did have choices. He was not forced into having an affair. He made that choice.

She could have made a bigger effort to get out, perhaps get another job or attend some classes. But it is only her that considers herself as a failure in this marriage.

Her daughter may see the marriage breakdown as a lesson in life. While upset with the outcome she may consider it is important to keep up social interests through a job and to work on the marriage with her future husband. Some experiences cause pain, others will empower.

Every experience can teach us something if we allow it. If we are receptive to being a student of life, then the world can deliver some invaluable lessons.

Failure is a pathetic disease that if we let it ruin our lives, it can destroy us. It doesn't really exist. It's a figment of our imagination until our thoughts add weight to it. Then it becomes disempowering and can cripple us.

I understand that if you were to invest your life savings into a macadamia nut farm in the middle of the Sahara Desert and you lost all your money, you might consider yourself a failure. I would say you are stupid at least but not a failure. You still have the ability to earn money, even if you are seventy-six. But that's another conversation or book.

The lesson here is look at what you did to get yourself in this position. The macadamia plantation scheme being promoted by L'iar 'N De'Shonko Investment Group offering a twenty one percent return on your investment (or would gamble be a better word) should have set off alarm bells in your head.

Greed may have blinded you in this case but if you learn the lesson of 'if it sounds too good to be true, it probably is' then you won't repeat it next time. You may also be able to school your friends in what to look for in bad investment proposals. And that would be kind of cool, wouldn't it?

Let's keep our minds in a more productive and proactive state and give up on holding lifelong pity parties. With better thoughts, we'll experience better feelings that will lead to having a stronger belief system. Positive beliefs create positive action which in turn creates better results.

So, in any situation look for the lesson. Overcome the problem, don't let it overcome you.

DAY 5
STOP SHOOTING YOURSELF IN THE FOOT

Ok it's time to move. Grab this book and move into the bathroom and look into the mirror. What do you see?

If you've answered George Clooney or Angelina Jolie that's great that you have such a positive opinion of yourself or perhaps you secretly wish these two super spunks actually were in your bathroom. Splash your face with cold water and let's get back to the real story at hand.

Some of you sighed when you stared into the mirror, didn't you? Are you a little bit fed up of the image you saw? Did you think dickhead? This conversation is going great; not.

If you are little bit fed up with yourself or thought 'what a dickhead', you're not alone. We all get tired of ourselves at some point. The trick is not to linger here too long. Self-sabotage is not smart. It's actually quite dumb.

How about making mistakes? Are there one or so mistakes you keep on making and wondering why things aren't changing?

Like knocking back a thick caramel milkshake and hot dog from Wendy's after your gym workout and wondering why you're not losing weight. You may laugh but I know people who eat a vegetarian pizza from Pizza Hut and wash it down with a diet Coke thinking that's healthy. Are they mad!

Here's something even crazier. They keep on repeating the same thing and getting the same result. No weight loss. So, how's that working for them? Quite clearly, it's not.

Human beings are amazing. They can be brilliant and stupid all at the same time. They then question the universe as to why things aren't changing, usually with their best goofy, victim face on. Everybody has the opportunity to be outstanding. But there's just one thing that gets in the way.

You and your lousy thinking. Ok there are two things for all you anal types who are currently saying "you said one thing". Get over it Princesses or you'll miss the lesson.

Are you still in front of your mirror? Get back there if you are not. Take a deep hard look. And don't start thinking "look at all those lines" girls.

Did you know that 43% of women in America have dated or are dating younger men? And the percentage is increasing. Why? Younger men see those lines as laughter lines. They see experience;

something younger girls can't give them and they want that. But I digress.

Your biggest challenge when you get up each morning is to stop the negative self-talk when you look in the mirror.

So, you're going a little bald 'Joe', shaved heads are sexy according to Cosmopolitan magazine. Don't let this negative self-talk become part of your self-sabotaging daily mantra.

Self-sabotage comes in many forms in addition to negative ruminating thoughts.

Procrastination will stop you living a full life as it robs you of the greatest asset around; opportunity.

Self-doubt or poor self-esteem is another form of self-sabotage that will cripple you. Too often we succumb to our thoughts or others and easily give away our power. "This will be the last piece of sponge cake I'll ever eat" until the next time at least.

How's the expression on your face? Any 'ah ha' looks?

Here's the thing. You can continue to go down the self-sabotaging path by shooting yourself in the foot by not learning the defeatist lesson or you can make a change. And speaking of shooting yourself in the foot are you using a pistol or a double-barreled shotgun? In either case it's pretty painful, so let's stop it now.

You can create a pretty amazing future. Be yourself and use your own great talents. You don't have to be like somebody else. Remember they are taken, just be you.

Stop over analyzing everything to the tenth degree and just start doing. Hey if 51% of your decisions are correct, you are in front.

Remember we've already discussed that there is no right time. Just do it now.

Stop being a people pleaser. You can't please all the people all the time. Please yourself first, some will follow, others will walk away. Next.

So put the self-sabotaging 'gun' down and start telling yourself how amazing you really are.

DAY 6

OPPORTUNITY DOESN'T KNOCK

I don't know about you; I've hung around a lot of doors. Experience tells me that opportunity doesn't come knocking. I don't know why that is but maybe the 'Big O' is shy, is not outgoing or doesn't like approaching strangers.

For me a knock on the door usually meant it was a debtor requiring money or some pesky neighbor wanting to borrow something.

I've always found opportunity to be a little inconspicuous. There's no fanfare, trumpets blazing or grand announcement. It's not wrapped up in a bow or dressed like Carmen Miranda.

Nope. For me opportunity has been something that either sneaks up on you arriving unannounced.

For most people they don't recognize it until sometime down the track. A mate of mine told me about a mentor of his who was starting a new company back in 1980. This mentor, we'll call him 'Jack' convinced sixty-six people to get into business with him during his first six months of set up. Unfortunately, fifty-seven of those quit.

Today the original nine who stayed and saw an opportunity, sit on top of a $5 billion company from which they are paid a percentage of the royalties. As for the other fifty-seven, who cares?

Opportunity is therefore hard to recognize. Sometimes it appears as a problem that once solved turns into an amazing opportunity. Sometimes it sitting in the wings, watching us, before it really appears.

I'm reminded of a Tasmanian girl called Mary who had to be coaxed by her friends to go out for a drink at a local bar. Begrudgingly she went and met a Prince and today she is Princess Mary of Denmark. What seemed to be an insignificant event turned out to be a life changing one for Mary Donaldson.

But we can't always blame opportunity itself for being missed. We humans have to be responsible as well.

Unfortunately, most people see opportunity as something requiring commitment whether it's financial or something worse; work!

Opportunity should come with no strings, a freebie. An opportunity may arise to earn some additional money. It may come in the form of overtime which in turn could lead to a promotion.

But if the opportunity is delivered in a quiet manner, without fuss, the event may seem insignificant and the person may choose to leave early and go to the pub with his mates. Six months later however the guy who gave up the chance maybe wondering how the 'newbie on the team, the guy with the least experience' got the promotion to manager. Opportunity doesn't always smack you in the face.

A lot of people however will continue to wait. They'll dismiss the newbie's promotion as being lucky and will continue on their merry way. They will wait for the free ride to come along because they don't want to pay the price. They rest their financial future on winning lotto rather than doing a bit extra and putting something away for a rainy day.

But it is very easy to change and get in tune with opportunity. Instead of waiting you just need to start doing. Get focused, make a decision, commit to doing the work and take action.

The funny thing is that opportunity will find you. You become an attraction magnet for the stuff. (That last sentence will keep all my "The Secret" mates happy; albeit most will remain in the closet).

Every week hundreds of millions of dollars are invested (I was going to say gambled) into the lottery. In Australia you can buy a ticket to win

Lotto six nights a week. Can you imagine that? Millions of people glued to their television sets watching and praying that their numbers will drop tonight. One person may win; the others will say "It's not my time – next week". Imagine having your whole existence dependent on a one in fifty-four million chance of winning the Lotto. Are you f*ckin' crazy!

The same people will tell you they can't afford to invest another $20/week into their Super because it'll cut into their smoke's money. Instead of quitting the dirty filthy habit, getting off their arses and creating a better life for themselves, they continue to wait for the 'one thing' that will change everything.

Ladies and gentlemen, opportunity isn't going to knock on your door. You're going to have to go out and find it or create it. If you want to move out of your crappy flat and buy your first home, get a better paying job or at least a second part time one.

Instead of watching the Powerball drop at 8.45pm, put the time into your work at home candle making business that you can sell online or at the markets this weekend.

So, what about you? Are you creating your opportunities?

DAY 7
DON'T FOLLOW THE HERD

Herd mentality is rife. The fear of being singled out particularly in this country is alive and well (or unwell depending on your view). While countries like America cheer on their success stories, Australians have a tendency to want to knock those who are seemingly successful. Aussies like to bring the stand outs back into the herd. It's called the 'tall poppy syndrome' and it's prevalent in our society.

One of the main downfalls of being a fully paid-up member of a herd is that you need to dispel your own personality. Individualism is frowned upon in a herd. You have to look the same, where the same type of clothing, speak the same lingo and generally be part of the crowd. Some companies promote the herd mentality.

This herd mentality thing can be a little covert as well. You don't realize it's happening to you. But given time, you start to become one of them. Your mannerisms change and you adopt the herd's beliefs and thinking, sometimes unintentionally and unconsciously. Scary, eh? Don't worry you won't feel a thing.

Let's go back to that mirror. Have a close look. Why are you here? By that I mean why are you on Planet Earth? To be like everybody else? No! Your purpose in to discover who you are and to project that person into the world. The world is a wonderful mix of individuals operating on this planet.

Of course, not all herds are bad. Some can be empowering. Some can help develop you as a person and therefore make the world a better place. Whether it be a sporting group, political or church group, if it empowers then it is worthwhile being a member.

But if you start to lose your identity, get out. Cults tend to operate best using the herd mentality. Strip away your individual traits and have you conform to group pressure. Those who break free of such groups eventually realize that this is what has been happening to them and they escape.

You arrived in this world as an individual and you should live your life as one.

Give the herd mentality a miss.

DAY 8
DON'T BE A QUITTER

You've probably heard this quote "Quitters never win AND Winners never quit".

That's a pretty true statement for the basic simple reason that quitters never finish anything. The task is always partly done but never concluded.

Winning isn't about having the best plan or the greatest of intentions, it's about doing. You need to put one foot in front of the other and to keep going. And that's difficult at times. Not every day is a bright happy day and you just don't feel like doing stuff. I get it but you just have to punch through it.

Too many people simply don't have a strong enough reason to do something. They fail to make decisions and just float around on a whim.

Successful people have that long term vision. Their plans match their values and they keep the big picture in front of themselves all the time, even after the initial bit of excitement has well and truly passed.

Are you prepared to put a bit of skin in the games, get out of your comfort zone or are you wanting quick, easy instant results?

Gyms are great places where people gather looking for fast results then quitting a month later when they don't look like Arnie. Gym owners love it because they've secured a full year's membership off you and you're now not using their equipment for the next eleven months. Sweet!

At the beginning of every year millions of people sit down to think about (the more serious ones write them down) their goals for the year. As a generalization they want to make changes in their life.

But for the majority come December of that year, they are still in the same place. The scales are still telling the same story, hopefully not a worse one. Once again, they've almost changed.

In January their intentions were great. They filled out their goals while listening to a replay of Rocky for the forty seventh time. They were pumped.

They needed to lose weight because their brother George is getting married in July. July rocks around and guess what? They are at the department store buying a larger suit because they quit on their diet and exercise plan back in February. They justify it by telling themselves that it didn't really matter as it was George's third wedding anyway and based on his track record, they would have another opportunity to slim down in about eighteen months.

Here's one thing you can't get back. It Is called time. You can apply your wish washy, weak kneed approach to life thinking that you can always do it tomorrow. Yeah right! You haven't adopted a well-balanced eating and exercising plan for forty years, why is everything going to change tomorrow.

You keep putting if off and without realizing it you'll be turning fifty or even worse sixty. If you thought things were tough at forty, wait to you add another ten years. The body doesn't move as well at fifty if you've been living a sedentary life.

We've all said it "If I had just stuck to that diet, I'd be 5 kilos lighter now". But we continue to go down the same merry path year after year.

How many times have you quit on something? That part time online eBay selling business could have been a raging success if you just stuck at it.

Yes, you may have had to fine tune your skills, take some courses and invest in yourself but that would have been better than still working for that prick boss who underpays you, right?

Every time you quit you go back to the beginning until the next time you get a spurt of motivation. Think about it. It'll wear you out.

It's time to stop quitting! Quitters never win and winners never quit!

DAY 9

OVERCOMING EMOTIONAL BURNOUT

Everybody has emotional highs and lows, managing them is the key. Positive emotions can spur us on to higher things but negative ones can cut us down in an instant. The mind is a very powerful thing and if not managed properly can lead to us having a pretty piss poor life. To the point, some people actually get sick.

We need to make better decisions. Too many people focus on the crap they can't fix. It's happened in the past and there's no way in hell that spending negative energy will ever turn the situation around. Get over it and move on. Negative energy will lead to burnout and we don't need it.

In order to make better decisions we need to be asking better questions. Instead of beating yourself up with a lump of timber with rusty nails protruding, we need to accept the wrongs of our past and ask how we could have done better. By using positive energy, a solution will appear from a seemingly hopeless situation.

One of the early signs that negative energy is taking hold of your life is the emergence of anger. You seem to be a normal person on the outside but the minutest thing can set you off into a rant or rage.

Anger however is usually covering up something a little deeper than appears on the surface. Fear can be a mask for anger.

If you perceive a colleague to be better than you may fear that person getting a promotion which in turn leads them earning more money, having a bigger house, faster car or a better looking, sexier partner. And they are not as good as you at their job.

Keep calm and don't allow those fears to ruminate in your head or you'll end up exploding, possibly in front of your boss which will probably ruin any chance of you getting promoted. It's a vicious little circle, isn't it?

Envy is another cover for anger. How come 'Alex' is the President of the club when 25 years ago he went down for fraud? Are you the only person in the world who knows that? Envy allows you to 'justify' your anger. People will admit to getting angry but never envious.

Complaining is another one of those masks of anger. Your golf buddy fires off a barrage of abuse complaining the only reason why his 'perfect' wedge shot onto the green is not closer to the hole is because the green keeper has no idea on how to mow a putting surface.

Equally the same guy complains that when his ball runs off the back of the green that the keeper cut the grass too short. After a tirade of complaining he vents his anger by slamming his wedge into the side of his buggy, bending the shaft in the process. Let's hope he doesn't need that club for the next fifteen holes.

<u>Blaming</u> is a bit like complaining as it requires you to take no responsibility for anything.

You bought a house forty kilometers from the city where there is no public transport. You don't have to be Einstein to figure out why you can't attract tenants to rent your home. It was all your own doing but for some reason you think it would be appropriate to blame the real estate agent who sold it to you.

Your dumb arse brother-in-law who is equally f*cked up as you, suggests you should sue the agent to get your money back. Assuming there's been no misrepresentation of the property you bought; you've got not a hope in harry of collecting a dime. And punching the wall won't bring a tenant in either.

Here's what we need to do to start managing our emotional energy to avoid burnout. Emotional energy flows from the inside out. We need to be better at talking to ourselves, store up our positive energy and let it flow out via our ideas and actions. That way we'll have a greater effect on the world.

DAY 10
WHO THE HECK ARE YOU?

One of the big questions we ask ourselves "Who am I?' It's one of those questions that can spark mixed emotions. Here's why.

Sit back for a few minutes, grab a piece of paper, a pencil (not a pen) and get yourself ready to make a list. Let's get your creative juices flowing by answering these questions.

Are you a Catholic? Do you believe in God? Are you a church goer? Are you involved in church activities like the choir, voluntary roles or do you play music at church?

Are you male or female? American or Australian or Asian or European? Are you working or retired? Are you unemployed? Do you work in an office or at home?

Did you go to college? How do you vote – Democrat or Republican, Liberal or Labor, Tory or Labor? Are you in favor of immigration?

Once you have a decent list, go through each point and eliminate them one by one. So, you eliminate that you are a Labor supporter. Does that now mean you are a Liberal fan? No, but perhaps you may see the other side of their philosophies.

You wrote down that you are a meat eater. Erasing this one doesn't mean you have to become a vegetarian.

So, what are we really doing? We are looking at ourselves without labels. It'll be a lightening of the mind, a sort of declutter. Keep going until you've eliminated everything on your list.

Now sit back, close your eyes and feel how empty you are. You'll feel more relaxed.

What was the purpose of doing this weird, crossed legged, kumbaya singing exercise?

Well after you've eliminated everything on your list, what's left?

YOU.

No matter how we label ourselves we still have us. Who the heck are you?

Labels don't really count. Self-confidence, our identity and happiness work from the inside out.

If we rely on labels (external stuff) to define ourselves, there will always be pain or anxiety. As we've just proven, strip away the labels and you still exist.

Now go conquer the world!

DAY 11
DISCOVER NEW EXPERIENCES

I know one thing about you. The fact that you bought this book tells me that you want to improve your life. Most people want to do better this year than they did last year. We want to change the way we think, feel, and act hopefully creating a positive change.

We know that to do this is an inside job. External things are superficial. What's the quickest, shortest way to create change?

In the last chapter we determined that material things don't really make up who we are. Strip them away and we are still left standing.

We are therefore a sum of all our experiences. If we want to change things, we need to change or add new experiences. The quickest way to change is to do things differently, experience different things.

Have you ever been sky diving? It's not on my bucket list but it would certainly be a different experience. There would be an instant feeling. To some that might be exhilaration. To others like me it would be instant fear. I would need to look at creating a shift in my mindset away from fear to one of excitement and adventure. In my case that may take some time, like a life time!

To discover new experiences, we can't just think them. We must do them. By doing we create a whole different dialogue with ourselves. What if your boss comes to you and says "I need you to go to New York this weekend for a conference"? This could be a new experience for you or not.

If you say to yourself "Aaagh I've got to go to f*ckin' New York this weekend" you are setting yourself up for a negative experience.

But if you change your thinking, and utter some different words like "I get to go to New York for the weekend" then you open up the possibilities for this experience to be positive.

Not only will you have the opportunity to learn something new, you may also meet new people, some of which can be great for your career. Boom more advancement and a pay rise. And you weren't going to go.

My nephew is a negative nelly. Always complaining that he doesn't have this or that. Life is hard according to Jim. To make himself feel better he signs up for a weeklong trip to Cambodia to help at an orphanage for street kids.

All of a sudden, his two-bedroom apartment, five hundred meters from the beach isn't too shabby after all. He gets to appreciate the little things he takes for granted like running, clean water and food on the table is not always the norm for some people in other countries.

Do different experiences and your life will change!

DAY 12
STOP TRYING TO CHANGE OTHERS

"Hey buddy, you're fat".

How much longer do you think I was able to live without sporting a black eye? Milliseconds and you'd probably be right.

Your over weight friend, parent or spouse may need to drop a few kilos. Don't we all. But did the person actually come to us and ask us how they could lose weight? Nope, I'm guessing not.

But we continue to offer our worldly advice to all and sundry thinking that it will be received with open arms and that we'll transform our recipient into a better person.

Sadly, it doesn't work like that. It probably says more about our need to feel wanted or important than actually helping another person. When the other person fails to recognize our good intentions, our feelings are hurt. Crazy! It's not supposed to be about us.

How do you respond when you're given unwanted advice? I used to be a smoker. My wife used to give me health warnings about smoking. I smoked even more trying to get through my anger.

Do you think the 'fat' guy you flood with your weight loss programme really puts down his jam donut and coke just because you became a Weight Watchers disciple?

No dickhead! He probably doubled his intake of sugar rich goodies just to spite you.

Jim Rohn has a great saying "In order for things to change, we've got to change"

So instead of trying to change everybody else perhaps we need to make some changes ourselves.

We can start by changing our response to things that displease us. Instead of preaching diet plans to everybody carrying an extra kilo or two, perhaps we need to accept who they are not what we think they should be.

Instead of ramming our views down somebody else's throat, perhaps we could offer some guidance once we are asked for help. That way there is no expectation that the person has to follow our recommendations. Aaagh the pressure is off.

Show others through our good example that we have life figured out. Eat a sensible diet, do some exercise and by doing that we will be the light for others to follow, if they choose.

The golden rule about trying to change people – don't. Unless you are asked for advice, don't offer your thoughts albeit given with the best intentions. Kids may be excluded from this group but tread warily with them.

Spend time working on the number one 'fix it up' case – YOU!

DAY 13
WHAT IS YOUR SUCCESS?

Everywhere you look you see that word 'success'. You read the local newspaper and a man is described as a successful businessman. Your flick through to the arty section of your weekend newspaper and some lady is described as a successful author.

Your mind wonders a little bit and you picture yourself in their shoes. The mansion on the hill, a Maserati in the garage and friends over for dinner at your twenty-four seat dining table.

This appears to be success but what is it exactly? Not sure?

If you can't define it, how will you know how to get it? You need clarity.

But is obtaining clarity real or a myth? You can have a big picture but perhaps it's necessary to break it down into bite sized chunks.

What kind of a family life defines success to you? What is the ideal successful job for you or should you run your own business? Who would be part of your closest friends for you to say that your life is successful?

While most of us tend to relate success to money or personal achievements, it's not really either of those. Every January a lot of people sit down and work out their goals for the year. It's their 'plan' to have a more successful life.

Let's say one of your goals for the upcoming year was to get into business for yourself. You start a mobile hot dog business, Harry's Supreme Hot Dogs. The business goes well and you attract some success.

You franchise your business and soon you have hundreds of hot dog vendors all over the country. Now you are a big-time success.

National Franchise Magazine puts you on the front cover and writes a feature article on you. You are living the dream. But on the other side of the fence, your customers are gaining weight. Your white buns are full of sugar which for some of your customers leads them to contracting diabetes. Are you still a success?

Perhaps you should just aim to be happy. You'd be successful, right? If your happiness is derived from people around you, then that may be fleeting. What happens when those people move away, die or just don't keep in contact?

Happiness is an internal thing anyway. This success thing is hard to define.

Living a healthy lifestyle can be construed as being successful. Eat good clean, healthy food. Exercise daily. Sounds simple doesn't. Success awaits. But what if that isn't enough to keep you motivated? What if you fall off the wagon? There's a lot of self-inflicted pressure to look good on the outside. Is this real success?

Success really is a personal thing. It's not universal. It's different for everybody. Some people will feel a total failure if they earn below $100,000 a year while another will be over the moon with $50k a year.

A sure-fire way to feel successful is to live in the moment. Get off your butt and start taking action. Little steps keep you moving forward. You are focused in the now and that helps create momentum.

Celebrate your little successes along the way. "I wrote five hundred words today!" The twenty percent you negotiated off your new washing machine is a success (for you at least. The washing machine salesman might think otherwise).

String a few small successes together and they add up to a big success. Success is what you define it. How does it taste, smell or feel? It's your personal choice.

Go grab your share today!

DAY 14
SUCK IT UP PRECIOUS

Ever looked at a boxer going into a world title fight and think to yourself; *I could do that*. It's only twelve three-minute rounds to collect a hundred million dollars. I'd do it for the money. I'd take a punch, lay down for the count of ten and collect my money.

Unfortunately, it doesn't work like that. The boxer has been doing weights, running a marathon each week and honing his craft for six hours a day for twelve months just to prepare for this fight.

Maybe boxing is a bit too violent for you. You watch Tiger Woods (replace him with another golfer if you don't like Mr. Woods' moral compass) approach the eighteen green to a standing ovation and think that could be you. Well, it could be if you had been practicing golf since you were three.

I once lived next to an Australian golfing professional who told me he hit one thousand golf balls a day to refine his game. Somedays I feel like I hit a thousand balls in a round, but every day; no way!

For a lot of people, it's easier to give up on these aspirations and settle for just fitting in. Being part of the norm. Just do what needs to be done, no more and no less (well less if you can get away with it, right?).

Everybody wants to be part of a tribe. People like to fit in. Standing out is frowned upon so it's best to copy the others and keep within the tribe. Soon our casualness leads to casualties.

We decide to hold our thoughts during a sales meeting even if the 'jumped up, four foot six, jerk sales manager' is completely wrong about the content he is delivering (oops I bashed another male sales manager – I'll have to use a female manager in the next chapter to balance things up).

Holding such thoughts in at work leads to one of two things. You fester about your working environment, start to self-sabotage your career, and soon you are in the unemployment que or you carry the same pattern home to your spouse and stifle your relationship.

But here's the weird thing. While we are trying to fit in with the 'normal crowd', do we ever ponder that there might be a better crowd? This attitude to conforming and staying in the same old crowd because you feel comfortable is B.S.

Too many people worry what the old crowd will think of them if they become 'too big for their boots'. Who gives a 'rats' anyway when you have the opportunity to join a better tribe?

But the better tribe will require you to step up. You may need to take a few risks or fifty. You may need to put your neck on the line (or your balls in the vice) to improve.

Life's an evolving thing. We don't really step out of our comfort zone but strengthen our tolerance to discomfort. This discomfort comes in many forms like financial stress, emotional pain or physical duress but if we are in tune with ourselves, we'll welcome them as lessons.

These lessons, provided they are learned, will teach us how to move forward, experience growth and gain more power.

Too many of us settle for the easy club where entry isn't hard. Do you know a conman's favorite hunting club – the normal one? The one where members can invest their superannuation into a scheme paying 27% per annum.

You don't have to be a financial expert; your new found wealth, advising friend will do everything for you. It's sad seeing seventy-nine-year old's packing groceries at the supermarket, isn't it?

Diet peddlers offer an easy fix for those who hate good eating and exercise. Pop a pill and the fat will melt away even if you sit on the couch hoovering down a peperoni pizza and a Pepsi seven days a week. Who are you kidding, Jack?

Sadly, we can rationalize anything if it means we can get out of creating discomfort in our lives. Unfortunately, we stay the same. Overweight and broke are two side effects of being comfortable.

Do the work Precious. Stretch that comfort zone. A better world awaits you.

DAY 15
STOP BEING A PEOPLE PLEASER

"I love to please people". "I'll do anything to make somebody else happy".

Really?

Who are you? Madame Needy? (told you I'd balance the books from the last chapter)

Are you really trying to please others or are you wanting to be liked? Deep down (or possibly closer to the surface than you think) it's more likely the latter.

Here's a quick test.

You give an expensive gift to a friend for their birthday. You wait by your mailbox for three weeks looking for the thank you card from your friend. You imagine it will arrive any day soon and be full of ten letter adjectives describing how wonderful your gift was.

By week four there's still no card. By week six you completely disown your friend. Taking away the fact that your friend shows little manners by not responding to well-wishers with a thank you card to anybody, did you really give the gift for the benefit of your friend or was it so that you can receive heaps of praise. Maybe the latter?

Ever give a talk to a group and receive a standing ovation at the end? But when you read the evaluation sheets on your performance, you notice there are fourteen high appraisals and one negative comment. Which is the one you remember?

Fourteen positive comments and a standing ovation counts for nothing in the eyes of a serial approval seeker when one tiny, little negative comment makes its way into the pile. Boom all the good stuff is forgotten and you are in a state of depression.

This is a total waste of your energy. Focusing on the negative, giving it power. The negative comment is most likely delivered anonymously. There is no way to validate it let alone ask the person for more clarity.

Writers have to deal a lot with masked negative reviewers. An author may get a ton of four- and five-star reviews but it'll be the one-star review that knocks him for six.

An author friend of mine, C T Mitchell, never reads the one- or two-star reviews. In his mind they are delivered by bitter little people who offer nothing. He refers to them as 'oxygen thief's'. Three-star reviewers and above offer a writer the opportunity to improve his or her craft, and those reviews are fondly received.

There's a saying that 'you can't please all the people all the time'. That's very true.

There's one person you should however always try to please and that's yourself.

You can pretend to try to please everybody but the only person who will ultimately suffer is you. Somewhere along the way your beliefs or values will be challenged.

It's not worth lowering them for the sake of being liked.

Understand who you are. What values do you hold most? It won't always be easy to live by them. You may feel periods of discomfort. Perhaps your world maybe confrontational. But that's ok.

It's more important to be your true self rather than Miss Needy. Live life on your terms, not those of others.

DAY 16
HAVE FUN

"Good morning Captain Serious". No time for fun today because you need to put your 'I'm serious, I'm focused and way too busy to have fun' face on to the outside world so they will take you seriously Mr. Businessman.

The morning news shows are full of stern looking CEO's trying to convince us that they are serious about fixing the problems of the world. Crikey, these grumpy sacks are on a million bucks a year plus and they can't look happy. Baloney!

Too many people are too busy, too important and too smart to have fun. They want to wait to they reach their goals before they give themselves permission to have some fun. Boring!

What if their goals change? What happens to the fun machine if the economy slips or even worse goes into recession? Do they put fun off for a year or ten? Imagine living with this dude. It must be a real fun palace at home.

Fun is all around us. It won't necessarily come to you. Sometimes you have got to go out and find it. And if you are having difficulties finding it, then you may have to create it yourself.

My next-door neighbor Mick just completed a wood turning course at TAFE. He's 79 and now he's making kids toys for Christmas. He's having so much fun he wishes he had started years ago.

Fun starts with your thinking. Are you receptive to new things? Are you keen to get involved in life? If it's not part of your natural make up then you'll have to commit to change. You need to have a curious mind. One that loves mixing with people, getting to know them and being involved. It's not much fun being a hermit.

But I understand life is not all about smiles, laughter and back slapping. There will be things that will test you. Life does throw a number of curve balls and it's not easy to put a smiley face on. But if you've been building your bank of fun experiences, you'll have some credits in store for when hardships happen. It's ok to make a withdrawal every now and then.

Scientists will tell us that people who engage in fun live better, have a healthier disposition and recover from illness quicker.

Call it the placebo effect, people who engage in regular fun things have fewer sick days and when they are struck down with something like the flu, seem to recover faster.

Fun is a necessary ingredient for your wellbeing. Find it, create it but make sure you get your share!

DAY 17
IMPROVEMENT OVER PERFECTION

I once read an article that said if you are not striving for perfection, you are accepting imperfection. I'm ok with that but the author wrote it with negative feelings. She meant that the acceptor of imperfection is willing to embrace a mediocre life. That's crap!

The article was in one of those self-help journals. I think it should have been in the self-hurt magazine instead.

This notion that we must have the perfect body, perfect mind, get perfect grades at school, have the perfect family is absolute crap and exhausting. I'm worn out just typing this shit.

What f*cked up jerk put this notion into our head in the first place. Give me their address, I want to bash them. Sorry, I'll calm down but people riddled with the perfection disease really sadden me.

A friend of mine said to me that if she had a million dollars right now her life would be perfect. I told her that I'd write her a cheque for a million bucks (I didn't have it. Yes, I was lying) and asked her if that would solve all her problems. She quickly replied "Yes".

I disagreed and told her that she would find something else that would make her life imperfect.

By then she had worked out that I didn't have the million and stormed off.

We seem to put things into our head that life will be perfect when we hit a goal. Bloody goals are the killer for most people not achieving stuff.

I once told myself that my life would be perfect when I became Director of Sales for a large Asian real estate group. It didn't happen.

I wanted to be a professional tennis player. Didn't happen. I wanted to date Elle McPherson. Never happened.

I read books on how to be perfect. Do this skill for 10,000 hours and you'll be a champion. Such reading set me on a course of destruction. Get good grades, go to Uni, get a good job, a mortgage and you'll live a perfect life. B.S!

What I've worked out that this world is a circus and that I was a performer. Every day I would practice trying to achieve the perfect act. Perfect act for the outside world. "Look at him with the nice house, Merc in the garage and Versace suits". The circus masters had me jumping through more and more hoops to try to hit my level of perfection.

I don't know about you, but when I go to a circus I like to be in the audience. I loved watching the clowns. But interestingly I never really knew who the clowns were. Unlike the lion tamer or the trick horseman, the clowns wore masks and make up which made it impossible to determine who they really were.

That's a bit like life isn't it. Who are the clowns in your life that keep pushing your perfection button? Are they worth it?

To be perfect we live a life determined by labels. We pretend to our friends and neighbours that we have the perfect marriage otherwise it's construed that we must be a failure. We must be a size ten to be a perfect woman otherwise no man will ever desire us. Really? Spend five minutes at the local mall to know that one is not true.

Instead of perfection how about we aim for improvement. Little steps that create a better life. How about cutting the cigs down then out altogether? Better for your health and hip pocket. What about aiming for a 1% improvement each day. Imagine where you'll be in a year.

Improvement keeps you in line with your values. You don't have to jump through hoops for the circus performer in order to achieve his perfection. Life is all about you buddy, not trying to please somebody else.

DAY 18
AVOIDING TOXIC PEOPLE

Your mobile phone is ringing. You see it's 'that person'. The one that's about to drain every last ounce of life from your body. You have a choice. Answer the call or ignore it. You tell yourself that you are a good person or perhaps guilt comes into play and you decide to take the call. Thirty-seven minutes later you are subliminally walking over the Brooklyn Bridge ready to jump.

Toxic people live for drama and are super keen to share it. It's their identity. Without it they are lost. When their world is peachy, they feel lost.

They quickly search for problems. If they can't find any of their own, they immerse themselves in other people's problems to the point they own the problem. If that's not cutting the mustard, they create the drama. The one thing toxic people really hate is calmness.

Toxic people are easy to spot. They stick out like the proverbial (ok dog's balls). There are generally four types of people in the world:

1. **The happy go lucky smiley types.** Sounds a bit cynical I know but there are some genuinely happy people. They seem to be always smiling even when they are having down days. Yes, they do have down days just like the rest of us but they know

how to handle the situation and navigate their way out of the problem.

But too much happy go lucky does get on some people's nerves. They resent these people and look to find chinks in their armor. They are on a mission to bring them down to their normal level or bury them deep into their own negative lives.

Resentment for the latter is a sport and they search for that flaw with vengeance.

In a world where there's not a lot of genuine happiness let's be positive about happy people and accept them for who they are, happy.

2. **People who genuinely suffer**. Unfortunately, there are those who do experience a lot of pain in their lives. They have a sickness, suffer cancer or have a physical issue. We need to feel compassion for these people. They don't peddle the 'woe - is - me' story and for a lot of the time convey a reasonably happy persona accepting their plight and deciding to live their life to the fullest.

3. **Good people are not always happy people**. They want to do good in society but can attract a similar brush of resentment from others. We don't need to be suspicious of all good people and we

should welcome with open arms them into our lives. There's not always a sinister motive attached to their doing good.

4. **Crappy people aren't good**. I know the tag gives them away but they are more cunning. They appear nice on the surface but are evil underneath. You know the types.

You will have some in your circle right now. They gossip about others. They suck you into the conversation. To be 'nice' you join in adding more fuel to their shitty fire.

But guess what? Once they leave and join another crowd, you are probably at the center of their snide comments. They appear to be popular but have no real friends. Avoid them like the plague.

Don't slip into the false belief you can help toxic people either. They are not after solutions. They just want to vent their opinion. They love the sound of their own voice. You'll be lucky to get a word into the conversation and if you do, you'll be immediately talked over.

But if you do fall into the illusion that you can help them with a bit of logic, brace yourself for their come back. They'll justify their position and lay blame elsewhere by offering excuses as to why they are different and how your logical argument won't work for them.

Toxic people will drag you down to their level; then beat you with experience. If your phone is ringing, don't take the call from 'Tommy or Tina Toxic'.

They'll soon move on to destroy somebody else's life.

DAY 19
BE FLEXIBLE

Change can be one of the greatest fears some people face. But being too stiff or rigid can be costly. In order to be relevant now in life or business, a person needs to adapt to change. It could be the difference between success or failure, business growth or decline.

To embrace change a person must first think differently and be prepared to act accordingly. They must want to change, have the ability to see it through and when adversity rears its ugly head, punch their way through the barrier.

Flexible people typically see opportunity where others see failure. Kodak dominated the film processing business. But when the world started to embrace the digital space, Kodak scoffed at the idea and remained rigid. And we know what happened to Kodak? The taxi industry and Uber are another interesting comparison.

Whining is not part of a flexible person's makeup either. If something is not working out, they adapt and move on.

Flexible people are not fully paid up, card carrying members of the 'blame club 'either. They take responsibility and deal with issues themselves. They learn from their mistakes, adapt and improve.

People who easily adapt have a curious mind. They are always seeking out ways or other people who can help them improve. Typically, they are the ones asking a lot of questions rather than telling you how great they are. The show ponies always talk "I, I". Boring!

Flexible people have better self-awareness. They know their values, what's important to them and what's not. Their path of progression is easy for them to map out.

Being flexible therefore opens up the world of more opportunities. Lose the blinkers and grow.

DAY 20
BETTER QUESTIONS GET BETTER ANSWERS

What kind of questions are you asking Champion? Ones that put you into a creative, positive, happy space or the woe-is-me type ones? We all have to deal with the latter but we need to be conscious on how to get ourselves into a better state.

Instead of asking yourself "What caused this failure?", how about asking, "How can I learn from this incident?". Your self-talk is critical. You need to be finding the positives in order for you to advance.

Questions are obviously not limited to the ones you ask yourself. They are a great way to find out information or build relationships with others. Here are a few things to look for in asking better questions.

1. **Before you ask a question, have you thought ahead**? If you are trying to get to a particular place in a conversation, are you leading the questions to that place or are you adopting an ad-hoc approach.
2. Good interviewers know where the conversation is heading. Michael Parkinson could lead a guest down a path without them knowing it. The audience was engaged and loving it.

3. **Don't ask questions that evoke a yes or no answer**. Such answers stifle a conversation and move the power away from you to the person answering. Your questions need to be more open ended.
4. As a person becomes more comfortable with you, they will be more open and offer up more information.
5. **Mix up the style of your questions and not always be delivering serious, pressing ones**. Be a bit light hearted which again will relax the interviewee.

Asking ourselves better questions generally leads to better results. When we are faced with a problem it is imperative that we stop for a moment, reflect and ask ourselves how we can best solve the issue. It's not the time to fire up, fly back at somebody with a barrage of abuse or tell the boss where he can stick his job.

Think before you speak. You'll ask more intelligent questions that will produce better answers and you'll keep your job longer (if that's your desire).

DAY 21
CHOOSING WHAT'S RIGHT FOR YOU

Since you've opened your biddy little eyes to the world, you've been told how to react based on what the advisor believes is right or wrong. This usually meant Mum and Dad. Sometimes grandparents, uncles, aunts or your next-door neighbour all threw their two bobs worth in.

Some of this advice had a biblical background. "Thou shall not steal" comes to mind later as a fourteen-year-old when you are pinching a Hershey bar from the corner store.

Depending on your parents' upbringing and the era in which they were raised you have been told the right way to speak, eat, communicate with your elders or study at school.

After enduring a mega download of advice from your parents between 3pm and 8am the next day, you then toddled off to school to listen to more advice on what is right or wrong from your teacher.

And if that wasn't enough free advice, you then jumped onto the computer and go a whole lot more advice from your favorite internet guru (is that me?), your Facebook buddies or that hot girl on Tinder (dating site?).

Tips on what's right or wrong never stop. They are thrust down your throat 24/7. But sometimes we need to take a step back and evaluate who is giving this advice.

Is it somebody who we respect?

Not every human being can know everything. It would be impossible to determine what is right or wrong just by taking counsel from one person. Do our values match those of that person? What events shaped their opinions? Are those events still current or valid today?

Most of the advice we receive on what's right or wrong has been fashioned by the values of the person delivering it or shaped by events in their lives. Such events may have had a profound positive or negative effect on how they thought from that moment forward.

Advice given is typically somebody's opinion on a subject. What's right for one person may not be so for another. There will be times when you are obliged to accept somebody else's right so as to keep the peace or appear to be a corporate team player even thought this right maybe one of your wrongs.

Rights and wrongs can also differ in different countries. What's considered right in Russia may be viewed completely differently in the US; wrong even.

There is no absolute right and wrong. As an individual you need to determine what's right and what's wrong for you. Even laws or rules can be determined differently as right or wrong. Unfortunately, your interpretation may not be accepted if you break them though.

Listen to what is right or wrong. Draw upon your childhood experiences, cross reference them with your current circumstances and decide what is right or wrong for you.

Good luck.

DAY 22
STOP OVER THINKING STUFF

How's that little voice in your head? Is it chatting away quietly or making a lot of noise? I'm sure you, like most people have these little voices in your head tossing stuff around. Maybe you are trying to sort out a work issue with a pressing deadline or a money problem.

There are things in our lives for which we have control and there are those we don't. Over thinkers tend to focus on stuff they have no control over.

They over think what somebody said or didn't say. They ruminate about what they should be doing or not doing. Their mind slips into the past regularly about stuff they can't change.

Thinking can be helpful, over thinking can be unhealthy. Over thinking can lead to negative thoughts.

Given power these thoughts become your reality. You can start second guessing yourself which in turn can lead to paralysis and nothing gets done. Fear takes over your life and soon everything is spiraling out of control.

How can you stop over thinking?

The simple answer is to stop thinking, initially for small periods at a time. This can be peaceful, invigorating and re-energizing. But if this congers up images of you wearing a sarong while sitting crossed legged on the floor with burning incense in the background and that's not your thing, then maybe these practical steps may help. But don't over think them.

1. Acknowledge that you are an over thinker and that you have to do something about it especially if your ruminating is causing anxiety and leading you into depression.

2. Calm yourself with breathing. Deep breaths will slow your heart rate giving you a sense of calmness and peace.

3. Don't ruminate with another ruminator. Some people want to talk through their issues. That's fine but seek out a professional. A friend may have good intentions but how do you know if your friend is not an over thinker as well. Two over thinkers together can be disastrous.

4. Get outside and exercise. Get out of the house, smell the air, feel the sunshine and go for a walk. If you are more physically fit, go for a run or do something that will raise your heartbeat even higher like swimming or

boxing. Exercise releases good endorphins which will help to create a positive mindset.
5. <u>Get busy.</u> Don't sit around in the dark and have negative conversations with yourself. Get busy with a hobby. Learn a new language. Take up guitar or learn to paint. Become active in something that you are passionate about.

Over thinking is such a waste of time and your talent. Do more. Act more. Be more.

DAY 23
YOU'RE NEVER TOO OLD

Ever hear somebody say "I'll soon be at the age to retire". Who says? Is there a rule that says you must retire by a certain age? I don't think so. Everything is a state of mind.

Prince Charles was once asked by one of the Spice Girls how old she thought he was. Geri replied "You're as old as the girl you feel and I'm 23". Prince Charles laughed but quickly removed his arm from her waist.

But there is an element of truth in that statement. Some people use age as a guide for how they should live. Society tells them old people play bowls while young skateboard.

When they were young, they wore hip, bright modern clothing. But once they declared themselves as old, they swapped the hip gear for plain, drab beige or brown seersucker trousers (and don't get me started on hat wearing male drivers…..).

Hogwash I say. Why do you have to be pigeon holed because of age? We often congratulate our twenty-year-old students when they graduate from university but give extra special attention to those who are older than their classmates. Can't we acccpt that this older person is just as capable as their fellow students?

Age is a thing of the mind. Those who think young tend to lead more vital lives thereby giving themselves a better chance to live longer. They see happiness and excitement in living and participate in life. They don't let opportunities pass them by. Who says an eighty-year-old can't go mountain climbing?

Dating and age is another one of those unstated discussions. A man dating a woman fifteen years his junior is considered successful, rich and possibly virile. A woman dating a younger man is often referred to as a cougar and is thought of in negative terms. That's hardly fair.

Who says that just because you've hit seventy five you need to trade in the Porsche Boxster for a sensible, small car like a Hyundai i30. There is no rule providing the seventy-five-year-old can pass a driving test.

Age can slow us down, if we let it. Living a healthy life which incorporates regular movement through exercise can sustain life beyond one's cutoff date.

Commit to living life to the fullest. Don't limit your fun and over all wellbeing by living your life according to societies view on how you should be living.

Stop acting your age. Age does not determine how you live.

DAY 24
WHAT'S YOUR REALITY?

Every day we are faced with various challenges. Depending on our reality, our perception of ourselves and the world, will determine how we react to such challenges. We are all different.

'Negative Norm' holds a master's degree in negativity. Whenever anything goes wrong for 'Norm' he rounds up his closest 'woe-is-me' mates and throws a pity party.

He sinks firmly into the problem. Being part of the solution is not on his radar.

Negativity defines Norm and he's not about to lose his identity by putting on an 'I'll be ok' face. It's also the perfect opportunity to recruit as many people as possible into the local branch of the 'nothing ever goes right for me' club.

If 'Norm' moans enough he may become the grand champion of the club; something that would make him very proud. In short 'Negative Norm' will suck the very last breath from you. Avoid him like the plague. Equally look out for his sister, 'Negative Nelly'.

'No fuss Nigel' is nothing like Norm. He's completely relaxed. Nothing fazes him. He's dealt some bad news, mulls it over for a few moments and then

pigeon holes it to be dealt with at a later time, if ever. This guy never stresses. He understands that some things can't be changed, so why waste time.

'Philosophical Pete' is the student of life always looking for the lesson. When he's faced with a challenge, he asks "what is the lesson I need to learn".

If it's a financial challenge, 'Pete' looks for ways to declutter his life. Scale back his expenses and get rid of stuff that's not really necessary at this time, although he'll never part with his Edward de Bono book collection. 'Pete' signs up for a bit of charity work so that he can justify his current predicament with 'there's always somebody worse off'. Thanks 'Pete'.

'Cranky Franky' blows at the drop of a hat. It doesn't take much to rile Frank up. He's always cranky. In fact, it's been so long; 'Cranky Franky' thinks he was born cranky. And he can prove it.

He's still mad at Johnny Pembleton who stole a kiss from Judy Sangster back in the third grade and he reminds himself every time one of his relationships falls apart. He carries his anger like a badge of honor but little does he realize that it has fueled his stress for the past forty-seven years, made him sick and lost him a lot of opportunities, including happiness.

But there are some people who shrug off challenges with ease. They get their fair share like most but have a different attitude to life. When a problem arises, they immediately ask themselves better questions. They are the half full type of person rather than seeing the glass half empty. Thank goodness these opportunists exist otherwise the world would be a very stagnant place.

We are all faced with challenges. It's not the challenge that is the problem. It's us. It's how we see the challenge and what we do next. We all have choices. We can choose to have a bad day or gone. It's our decision. Choose your reality wisely.

Your future, your life depends on it.

DAY 25
LIVING WITH PURPOSE

Living your life by your values, beliefs and with purpose can be quite difficult. You may want to bundle all these things into a simple batch and say that you need to live your life in balance. But balance to some means the relationship between your personal life and your professional life.

But living by values, beliefs and purpose goes much deeper than that. Oh, oh, here he goes with another mumbo jumbo, back slapping, foot stopping rendition of kumbaya while wearing kaftans and dancing around an open fire. No, but what color kaftan do you like?

Besides all the great singing and dancing, living your life in alignment can lead to a much happier life. Being able to make decisions based on our core values gives us a balanced life.

In the real world where we are influenced by so many external forces pulling us between pillar and post, we need to get ourselves in a position where we can consciously live our lives in harmony. Living in alignment with our values, beliefs and purpose will lead to a less stressful life. Stress is of your overall wellbeing and it needs to be curtailed.

Sure, we can coast long and see where life takes us but we may not like where we end up. Having a life purpose will definitely get us closer to an aligned life. Socrates said "Living an unexamined life is not worth living". (Hopefully Socrates was a smart bloke. With a name like that, he sounds smart, right?)

What is your purpose?

It's hard to define but you'll know by how you feel. If you are not empowered, enthused and excited everyday then you haven't found your purpose.

Big call I know but this is where you need to be headed. It's not going to happen tomorrow. It doesn't mean that life from here on out is bliss and you won't ever experience another negative moment. Nope. But it will mean that you will be living in a stronger place and that you'll be better armed to deal with negativity.

Having a purpose will be the beginning of life for you. Too often we pursue a life based on somebody else's dreams or what is perceived to be right for society. We busily go about setting goals and carrying out plans to arrive at a destination that is not what we were looking for in the first place.

By determining your purpose you'll be able to set better long-term goals, short term ones and create a daily action plan that is in alignment with your values and beliefs. That's why it's important to get clarity up front instead of pursuing things that will not bring you ultimate happiness.

With clarity you can then focus 80% of your efforts on the 20% of things that really matter and will make a difference in your life.

And let me burst the bubble right now about what some of you may be thinking. Money is not a life purpose! We are looking much deeper than that 'Rockefeller'.

Imagine the effect of living a life with purpose and how that will affect your career decisions. You won't be doing stuff to keep your boss happy while you are getting rewarded by a miniscule pay packet.

Instead by making your own choices you'll live a life of energy and passion. And when success does come (that'll be by your definition), it will be on your terms and not some 'fat cat' in the corner office getting rich. You'll be richer in so many more ways.

So how do you find your purpose?

Grab a piece of paper (ok notes on your iPhone or iPad will do 'Ms. Techno Whizz') and start writing down answers to "What is my life purpose?"

Jot down anything that comes to mind. Even if it sounds silly keep asking the question until you get to the answer that makes you cry (it's ok big boy to cry. Pappa won't tell your bikie mates).

Here's the secret to getting your thoughts down on paper. Write down what pops into your head. Don't judge based on what your think society would expect or want. Don't filter stuff out by thinking it's not relevant. If you are doubtful about it making the list, leave it. Don't eliminate.

Keep going to the point that something resonates. You'll know by the emotion it evokes. If it's the one that makes you cry, you've found your purpose.

Take your thought then re-write it into a positive action statement. "To bring self-confidence to mental health sufferers so they live a long, happy and passionate life"

Review this statement at least monthly but I would suggest each morning. Sitting quietly in a chair in a room by yourself and read this statement out loud a few times, then reflect on it for the next ten minutes.

This will give you the best start to your day!

DAY 26
WHEN YOUR BODY SPEAKS, LISTEN

The human body is an amazing machine. It functions usually all by itself. People have different attitudes towards their bodies. Some see it as a finely tuned machine like a top racing car and constantly look for ways to not only maintain it efficiently but to also improve its performance.

They fuel it with good quality food. They maintain it in peak condition by regularly exercising it. To this group of people, a well-maintained body is not taken for granted.

Then there's the couch potato group.

They couldn't care less about their bodies. They believe their body will last for a long time and then they'll die. A diet rich in fat supported by sugar drinks is the norm for them. Pizza Hut, Kentucky Fried Chicken and Coke-a-Cola are the global houses of fine cuisine.

Salads and seasonal vegetables cannot be found in the crisper in their fridges, except for when Grandma comes to visit. Stupidly they believe they'll live to ninety like grannie because it's in the genes.

Yes, they might be fat, overweight or even obese but they believe the God's will look after them. It's also normal for these 'heart attack waiting to happen' friends to consume a packet of cigarettes a day and four or five beers a night. The ciggies and grog never killed Uncle Jock, so it won't kill them either.

The government tries to help these people. They pour millions of dollars into anti-smoking campaigns, redesign cigarette packaging with people losing their limbs and as a final straw continue to raise prices around Budget time.

But 'Smokin' Joe' simply changes the telly when the ads come on, places his over-sized mit over the cigarette packet blocking out the images and alters his 'budget' by cutting back on his holiday fund, superannuation or kids' education fund. It's a tough world for the working man but there's no way he's giving up the fags or booze.

But what happens when he does get sick? Even before he rings the bulk billing doctor, he'll get one of the kids to Google his symptoms and self-diagnose himself.

Bloody Einstein at work!

But we don't have to live in extremes. There is a middle ground that can deliver a better life without having to resort to eating only lettuce leaves and not feel that you are missing out in life. We do however need to listen to our bodies if we want to enjoy life more though.

We should start taking note of any warning signs. If you are feeling lethargic, always yawning or tired then you need to make a note and visit your GP sooner than later.

It maybe something simple like adding more water to your diet. But if there is something sinister going on, your doctor will pick it up straight away.

Learning to relax more can be another way to improve your body.

A simple 10-minute meditation each morning is a great way to center yourself, energize your body and help you plough through the day. If you like something longer, sign up for some yoga classes which is ideal for your total wellness.

Food is the ultimate weapon in having an optimum body. Eat when you are hungry and avoid fatty or sugar rich foods. Water is the best liquid and it has no calories. Also try to eat in relaxed and peaceful surroundings. Turn the television off and savour your meal. Enjoy your company rather than the negative messages the seven o'clock news is pumping out.

We only have one body. Listen to it and it'll last a lot longer.

DAY 27
DON'T WASTE YOUR POTENTIAL

I once read a story of a woman, who weighed just 58 kilos, found the strength to lift a car off her trapped body. How is it possible that she could lift over 1500 kilos to free herself?

Perhaps the answer lies in her immense will to free herself. Perhaps it was more than that. Maybe she realized that she had to free herself as she was responsible to her family and the upbringing of her children. I don't know the answer but obviously it took a super human effort.

And that is the amazing thing about us humans. We can perform extraordinary things when we need to. If our backs are truly against the wall, a matter of life or death, then such an act is possible. It seems possible. We tend to have a shift in our mindset by moving from doubt to one of absolute belief.

It doesn't always have to be life or death situation. When challenged, some people are able to move past their fears or phobias and perform abnormal feats. They see no way out other than busting through the thing that has always held them back up until this point. They are determined not to let this obstacle block their lives any further and usually with such commitment, breakthrough the hurdle with ease.

Pity it takes a crisis to create the change.

But here's the fact about creating change. It wasn't the crisis that gave you the skills to handle it. Sure, it forced you to take action but the qualities and skills were already housed in you.

Up until this point you've chosen consciously or subconsciously not to do anything about it. You've decided to coast along accepting your fate. You've sat back and waited for things to happen and then when forced into a corner, you've reacted.

Imagine a guy running a real estate business drowning in debt. His choice is to make more sales, increase his rent roll so he can derive more income or sell the business and salvage what he can.

He chooses to do none of the above until the bank comes knocking. With 'blood in the water' he approaches his cash up competitors to buy him out. They know he's in trouble, bad news travels fast. They might be happy to stop the 'bleeding' but not save his life. Before too long the bank issues him a wind-up notice and the bargain hunters snap up his assets for just cents in the dollar.

What a pity it took a major crisis for the owner to act. Had he started the process months earlier, sought help, increased his sales team or started liquidating some of his rent roll to pacify the bank, he could have possibly saved his business.

Don't let your limiting self-beliefs or your over analyzing mind stop you from leading a full life.

The potential is already in you. Don't wait for a crisis to make a change. You can't change the past but you can certainly influence your future.

Don't waste your potential – use it now!

DAY 28
THE UNBREAKABLE MUST-DO'S

It's holiday time. Fantastic! You've worked hard all year and now it's time for a bit of relaxation. In choosing where you want to go, how long you want to stay and what you want to do once you are there, involves a number of decisions. Most of these decisions will be variable.

You can travel by car, train, bus or plane. You can stay in a 5-star hotel, an apartment or even a caravan park. You can book direct, use a discount travel site or jump on Airbnb. You have a number of options.

But there will be some decisions that are not negotiable. They require a firm decision. They are you must-do's. Actually, booking your travel is a must do if you want to holiday.

In life we also have a number of habits or behaviors that are absolutely non-negotiable when we are deciding where we want to go. It's the stuff we must do every single day if we want to achieve long term change.

Let's say you are a real estate agent wanting to become a million-dollar earner. In order to sell more properties, you'll need to find more buyers and sellers.

Prospecting for either or would be a non-negotiable habit that you would have to perform daily to achieve your goal.

Must do's are not luxuries. For a mother taking time out with friends away from her kids should not be considered a luxury or something she should feel guilty about.

It's an essential part of having balance in her life and it must be something that is non-negotiable. Yes, I know there may be a few tears from the kiddies when they are not invited to the local café with your girlfriends, but they'll just have to miss out on their babycino this time.

Non-negotiables don't need to be complicated. They may be difficult to do some days, like an early morning run because you want to get fit, but they are definitely not complicated. Just put one foot in front of the other Start walking or jogging, quicken the pace and you'll soon be running.

Your non-negotiables are your must-do's, nobody else's. They are necessary for you to achieve what you want and should not consider them to be selfish. We all need 'me time'.

Non-negotiables can be broken down into four basic categories which you can carry out on a daily basis.

In order for you to make your own list here are a few ideas (but for you they'll be non-negotiable):

Physical

- Wake up at 5.30am. It's that early bird catches the worm stuff.
- Exercise for 30 minutes. Start with a walk.
- Go to sleep by 9.30pm. You need your 8 hours of beauty sleep in spite of what hubby says. He has motives.

Emotional

- Don't engage with negative, life sucking people.
- Be honest. It's too hard to tell lies unless you have a great memory – and you don't!
- Express love and kindness with loved ones and friends.

Mental

- Read for 10-30 minutes when you wake up. Fill your head with something positive.
- Do a crossword

- Review the good things you achieved yesterday. Write in your gratitude journal

Spiritual

- Mediate. If you are just beginning, start with 10 minutes. Close your eyes and breathe deeply.
- Be grateful. Let others know including yourself.
- Talk to your God.

If you want to improve your life non-negotiables practiced on a daily basis are a must –do. <u>Start today!</u>

DAY 29
UNLEARN LIMITING BELIEFS

What if you discovered a belief you've held for 'centuries' simply isn't true? This may come as a crushing blow to some of you forty-seven-year-olds that Santa isn't really true. Ok that might be an exaggeration but you get what I mean.

For some people their 'truth' has been part of their whole make up for decades.

Questioning it is out of the …….. question. Why? Because it will shatter who they are. They would be mortified to discover that their long-held belief simply isn't true. It's safer to put up the barriers and to block out any thought of it ever being false.

People with these strongly held views tend to fire up and will defend their beliefs to the end of the Earth. They retort in an almost shouting way. They are out to convince you that you are the one with the wrong view and that they won't be giving up on their belief any time soon.

Beliefs give people some sense of surety. But if they were to discover that such a belief is false, then they will feel confused, lost or vulnerable. It can be quite unsettling to the point they feel betrayed especially to the person who originally plant the seed of that belief. (It's ok Mum – I forgive you about the Santa Claus thing).

So, if you are faced with such an issue and you are willing to accept another view, how do you move forward? Well, you need to unlearn that belief:

- **Accept that you may have learned things that are false.** We all make mistakes.
- **Did your belief empower you or limit you?** If it was the latter, ditch it.
- **Was this belief rammed down your throat by somebody else** until you took ownership of it yourself? If so, it's ok to question it and then decide to keep it or drop it.
- **Breakdown the belief into smaller chunks** and question every single component.

Beliefs determine our actions. Some empower, others take away. From our actions we get results. What do you need to unlearn? Start questioning today.

DAY 30
GET YOUR PRIORITIES RIGHT

Ever get to December 31 and reflect on your year? You know you've been putting effort in, doing stuff but what have you achieved? Are you more advanced than last year, about the same or have slipped down a couple of notches?

For some people they have been busy at being busy without really achieving very much. They are on the treadmill running flat out but actually aren't going anywhere. Ever feel like that?

Then it's perhaps time you looked at prioritizing things in your life.

A lot of us think that in order to achieve more, we need more going on. So, we try to juggle fifty balls in the air resulting in many of them hitting the ground with a thud, including us.

Come the summer holidays most of us are burnt out. We book a holiday and because we are addicted to this cramming as much into a day lifestyle, we book a fourteen-country cross Europe trip into seven days and arrive home exhausted.

Trying to cram your life with a gazillion things will only produce exhaustion, disappointment and de-motivation. You'll get to the end of the year with only a few ticks on the positive side of the ledger.

You need to take stock of the situation now. Next year is going to be different.

Drop the gazillion things for a few days, may be a week, step back, take a deep breath and start to prioritize what is really necessary for you to get to where you are really going.

Firstly, decide if your current approach is working. I'm guessing not. Make the decision to change. You've probably said that to yourself a million times, but today is the day. No more excuses. Your life depends on it. It's that serious.

Refer back to your must-do's that you wrote down in an earlier chapter (you did write them down, didn't you?).

For me I believe we all need to tackle our physical and mental health. Without a fully optimized body and mind it's difficult to sustain the energy for the long haul.

Eat right, do some exercise and fill your mind with positive stuff. Give yourself a good talking to everyday "I am feeling fit, toned and healthier every single day". But don't overload the system. Keep it simple.

Get plenty of sleep (8 hours a night) and unplug from technology before you go to bed. The body needs rest to rebuild.

Declutter your life including your mind. Most of us get hundreds of emails a day. Are they all that important that you can't unsubscribe to? Select a few that you actually read and dump the rest. Remember most of those 'business gurus' are just warming you up for another sale. Unsubscribe.

Now that you are getting a few of these things in shape, look at where you want to go. Is it to make more money, have a holiday or reduce some debt?

Pick one thing and break it down into manageable steps. If you want to go for a beach holiday next Christmas, decide where and work out the approximate investment you'll need to make to get there. Holidays aren't a cost; they are an investment in your wellbeing.

Prioritize the steps you need to achieve this. Earn more money by taking on more shifts at work, smooching to the boss for a pay rise or starting a part-time business. You don't have to be a work-a-holic rather a chooser of your own path.

Work out your priorities and stick to them. Don't be tempted by the shiny light promising you better things elsewhere. Your success lies in you doing stuff consistently now.

****

Over the past thirty days I've given you some strategies to create a better life. It's now up to you. This can be your last self-help book to get your life going in the right direction or you can continue to pour more dollars into stuff and not take action.

It's time 'Charlie'…..'Wilamena'…..stop f*cking around and get started! (and keep going!!)

THE LAST WORD (S)

You made it. Good on you!

You're in the minority. Most people don't read a book in its entirety.

You've now got thirty days of actionable steps to help you stop f*cking around.

That might be enough. Some of you will:

- Read this book at least 10 times
- Highlight paragraphs or chapters for easy future reference
- Some will take **ACTION.**

Others will need more help. Years ago, on a blog (now buried), I wrote an article called The 10 Rules I Live By. The main theme was getting things done; critical if you want to ditch the f*cking around tag.

It got a bucket load of likes. People emailed me and told me what a life changing piece it was.

Here's the 2021 version to finish off the book.

TEN RULES FOR NON-F*CKING AROUND TYPES TO LIVE BY

1. **Non – f*cking around types don't wait to things to happen**
   Dicks wait for things to happen. Smart types make things happen

2. **Deluded nuffties focus on sh*t they can't change**

3. **Verbal diarrhea types talk crap**
   Fully blown wankers talking about stuff that they never did or likely to do. Energy sappers – ELIMINATE!!

4. **Lose the upstart, smart arse, dickhead attitude**
   F*ckwits stink. An aggressive shit attitude gets you nowhere. You attract more flies with honey than vinegar

5. **Impotent, goal deprived losers leave everything to last**
   Bad idea. Do the tough stuff first and do it early.

6. **Sooky crybabies sulk**
   Bad things happen to everybody. Life is not fair. Get over yourself. Move on.

7. **Unmotivated dicks find difficulty in everything**
   Keep it simple Simon or Simone.

8. **Overweight Oscar's binge on crap**
   Get off the junk food. Eat more fruit and vegetables. Plant based diets are healthy, just ask a gorilla.

9. **F*cking around types major in limiting beliefs**
   Lose them. Tell yourself that you are ok.

10. **Ruminating Ronny over thinks stuff**
    Over thinking breaks momentum. Success is just about doing stuff consistently and putting one foot in front of the other

Good luck

www.ingramcontent.com/pod-product-compliance
Lightning Source LLC
Chambersburg PA
CBHW030258010526
44107CB00053B/1756